Praise for *In Deep Waters*

"I love this book. Aho is a beautiful writer, teacher, and ally of the young—wise and tender and tough. If you love young people and the earth, this might be the most important book you read this year."
—Anne Lamott, author of *Almost Everything: Notes on Hope*

"Most generations living on earth right now have a complacent attitude toward the looming climate crisis. For the most part, we think, it won't affect our lives in any serious way. But the younger generations do not have that luxury. The existential threat of climate change hangs over them, resulting in an unprecedented crisis of spirit as these generations try to imagine what their future might be like in such an unstable world. Talitha Amadea Aho's *In Deep Waters* is a masterfully written guide both for the younger generation as they grapple with the spiritual questions that emerge when contemplating the climate crisis and for those of us in older generations who need a reminder of the magnitude of the crisis we're facing and guidance on how to care well for the next generation."
—Brandan Robertson, author of *Filled to Be Emptied:
The Path to Liberation for Privileged People*

"*In Deep Waters* clearly and evocatively captures the complexities of growing up on the edge of apocalypse—with all the spiritual, emotional, and mental turmoil that entails. Talitha Amadea Aho's unique perspective provides insight into the generational dynamics of the climate crisis, as well as the paths we have in front of us if we are to journey on together."
—Zoe Jonick, youth climate activist and organizer

"Climate change has left an unjust burden on the youngest generations to organize and act in order to live. People of faith owe these youth and young adults bold spiritual support as we grapple with a bleak future. Aho's writing spurs us into collective action that honors the work to be done and tends the spirits of those who must do it."
—abby mohaupt, PCUSA pastor,
climate change activist, artist, and mama

IN DEEP WATERS

IN DEEP WATERS

Spiritual Care
for Young People
in a Climate Crisis

Talitha Amadea Aho

Fortress Press
Minneapolis

Cover design and illustration: Brad Norr Design

Print ISBN: 978-1-5064-6978-2
eBook ISBN: 978-1-5064-6979-9

Contents

Contents

Preface

It was three fire seasons ago, driving a van full of teenagers through thick smoke as we made our way out of the San Francisco Bay Area, that I first woke up to the apocalypse. It was not my ecological awakening; I was already an avid bicycler, recycler, and backyard composter. It was not my first spiritual awakening; I was already an ordained Presbyterian pastor. But that evening in 2018 as the sun set bloody red and the windshield wipers swept away ash, I had an awakening unlike any before. I listened to the angst of my young travel companions, and the alarm bells started ringing deep within my soul.

My travel companions, whom you will meet over the course of this book, gazed out of the van windows into the eerie haze and gave voice to the existential crisis of being teenagers in a world on fire. They vented their hopelessness and helplessness. They let loose their anger with God, the US government, and a few choice corporations. They shared their best strategies for coping with this ultimately un-cope-able reality. They talked and talked. And listening to them, I finally started to hear the bells ringing in the apocalypse.

Listening to those alarms—even tuning into them instead of shushing them—I have learned that they are not like sirens warning us to evacuate. They are more like the town bells that call the community to assemble; we run toward them, not away. They are a call to prayer. They invite us to litanies of grief and solemn vows of commitment. They call us to a more ecologically attuned spiritual life, rich with beauty and pain, attuned to the groans of all creation. They call us to action on behalf of the earth and the struggling people on it, especially those people most impacted by the toxic intersections of powerlessness and poverty. They call us to rise up and respond.

I would not have had this awakening without the company I keep: a brave bunch of Generation Z Californians whose eyes are wide open as they stare down the ecological abyss. This book is for them.

Names have been changed in some cases to protect the confidentiality of those who came to me for spiritual care. Note also that the young people I quote have been growing, learning, and changing over the few years it took to write this book; I honor their willingness to have their younger perspectives published, even as they continue to develop and articulate their ideas.

Introduction

On the sixth day, God gave the gift of creatures that
live on the land: those that walk on four legs, and
those that walk on two; those that walk on six legs
or eight or a hundred. And God made people, in
God's own image, and told them to take care of the
world.

Well, *that's* the day where God made a mistake.

—WILLIAM, eleven

The world as we know it is ending. Several millennia of climate stability have come to an abrupt end, and we are now in
an era of instability. Those who care are still fighting to "save
the world," but those with their eyes open realize that much
of the world is already beyond saving. Species have been lost
forever, ecosystems are changed beyond recognition, and there
is little hope of bringing temperatures back down to their his-
toric averages. People can still fight for a more livable future,
but we cannot fight to save it all; much of it is already lost. We

are at the end of the world as we know it. And sadly, we do not feel nearly as "fine" with this as REM prepared us to feel.

The young people of today do not know what the world was like before it was ending. They do not remember stability. Climate change has bloomed from a crisis into an all-alarm emergency before their eyes. Those of us who came of age before or around the millennium can remember back when climate change was an interesting thing to learn about in science class—we called it "global warming" back then and worried about CFCs and ozone. Well, not too long afterward, climate change made a jump from the realm of theory into sensational news stories, as record-breaking temperatures and storms in many places dominated our attention. But by now, no matter where you live, it has jumped out of the news and into real life. Here in the San Francisco Bay Area the climate emergency feels like heat and smells like wildfire smoke. In other places, it feels like rising water levels and smells like postflood mold and mildew.

The young people of today see the world through crisis-colored glasses. The illusion of stability is a foreign concept to Generation Z (born between 1995 and 2010). They know all too well how a virus can come along and rip the fabric of our society to shreds while forests burn and shorelines wash away, leaving human and nonhuman creatures bereft and mourning. The young people of today are well acquainted with what it feels like when the world is ending.

As seas and temperatures rise, people are rising too. Movements are swelling up to meet this moment, calling for a more just society that protects "the least of these," and working to put an end to the death-dealing ways that landed us in this mess. Activists have arisen who would have never called themselves activists before, as it becomes clear that we will not get out of this mess easily. People of all vocations see the challenging work laid out before them: advocating for systemic reform, moving to cleaner fuels, reducing our carbon footprints, conserving wild spaces and protecting vulnerable species, inventing new technologies, and preserving older (wiser) sustainable traditions. The climate crisis calls politicians, engineers, biologists, farmers, ranchers, architects, and homemakers alike. Poets and artists help us lament our ecological losses, while prophets keep alive the will to fight for a better tomorrow. Everyone has their different work. But no matter our vocation we share the anguish and the spiritual crisis. This work is hard. We hear the groaning of creation from human and nonhuman voices: the cry of grief, the grunt of labor, the shriek of pain, and the silence of death. We cannot hear these without being moved. We respond by getting braver, stronger, more emotionally open, and more committed to the work we must do. We respond by opening our hearts and minds to care for one another. We respond, that is, with a spiritual awakening.

Not too many years ago we would have said that the major threats to the health of the world were pollution, rising temperatures, and the loss of delicate ecosystems. But now we see that the greatest threats to our world are far subtler. They are selfishness, apathy, and greed. These are the root causes of the human destructive behaviors that lay waste our lands and pollute our seas; these are our sin.

Climate change is a faith-shaker. No longer can we naïvely hope that people will do the right thing: people have repeatedly failed to do it. And humanity's sin is on full display as the climate crisis pulls the curtain back to show us our selfish greed, systemic racism, and collective apathy.

The climate crisis is so huge and far-reaching that it cannot help but call us to repent and turn toward love for our human and nonhuman neighbors. And so all the work we do in our various vocations must be accompanied by this one universal vocation: we are all called to care for one another. A solo spirituality is seldom strong enough to lift us through perilous waters such as these. We need a communal spiritual practice that gives and takes; we need love handed from one person to another around the circle of community. We need the skills and habits and practices that are called "spiritual care." All of us need spiritual care and benefit from it. But we especially need to provide care for those who are in more powerless positions because of their youth—the children, youth, and young adults of Generation Z. We need to do it today; we cannot wait until they grow up.

> *Unless you change and become like children,*
> *you will never enter the kingdom of heaven.*
> —Matthew 18:3

The Gospels are clear: there's something special about young people. A reader cannot miss the way Jesus repeatedly calls children to him, blesses them, rebukes those who would stand in their way, and challenges his followers to pay attention to them. He tells the grown-ups to learn from the children and become more like them. For a probably childless man, traveling from town to town, who told his disciples to leave their families behind to follow him, he had a remarkable amount to say about children.

Churches love to parade cute kids around for everyone to "aww" at, but taking Jesus seriously means you really cannot just exploit their cuteness. It always backfires sometime or another, and when it does, it affects the children deeply. My first clear memory of church from my childhood was when, during a children's sermon, I raised my hand to answer a question that I took too literally. I remember what it felt like when the entire congregation laughed. That day I learned an unwanted lesson: I would not be welcome until I was a grown-up and knew how to answer these questions. But if we truly want to follow Jesus's radical and mysterious teachings about children, we need to treat younger people with awe and dignity, remembering that they have something valuable to teach us all.

Often people say children are "the future of the church." I try to take it graciously, but inwardly I cringe. Somehow this statement skips entirely over the gifts these young people have *now* and values them instead as containers of potential: as future adults, future workers, or even more cynically, future pledging units. But young people are not the future of the church; they are the present moment. They are here as fully spiritual, fully dimensional beings right now.

Young people have blessings to share, and by paying attention to them, we can receive some of those blessings.

They have so much joy, creativity, imagination. Youthful energy is invigorating, and being around people who are learning and growing as fast as they can is inspiring. The faith of a child who believes anything is possible is a breath of fresh air to those who have gotten cynical as they have grown up. We who are older intuitively want them to share these blessings with the world. Harder to accept is the truth that young people have warnings to share with the world as well as blessings. They have trouble to share. Because they see things differently, from their unique standpoint, and they experience feelings more urgently from their younger and more passionate brains and bodies. What's more, they can call bullshit when they see it. They have alarms to ring and distress cries to publish, and these are just as important as the blessings. We all need to take them seriously.

But a generation is coming of age right now, from the twelve-year-olds in our confirmation classes to the twenty-five-year-old graduate students, in a world that is not taking them very seriously. They are ridiculed and rejected for their youth yet simultaneously expected to save us all, and if they complain, they are told to chill. But chill, for young people today, is in notably short supply as the air around them warms.

> *Oh, the number of times that we're told "you're the generation that's going to fix it all!" But we don't have a choice. This is all or nothing. We either do something about it or something horrible happens. And obviously, horrible things are already happening. That's the thing we're facing*

> right now. It's not like "I want to be good," it's like
> "I literally just want to live until I'm eighty." And
> have kids and whatever, like future generations.
>
> —Justine, nineteen

The children in our church's Sunday school classroom heard the story of Creation and asked if it would not have been better if God had stopped on day five, before humans arrived. "Let's leave that part out of the story," they said, "before things went bad." If we never had humans, we would never have had war, or pollution, or climate change. Then the world could have been at peace, filled with creeping things and winged birds, and the seas unpolluted, and the skies clear.

The teenagers, more critical, are not sure if there even is a God, or if there is, they think God is asleep at the divine wheel. They wonder if humans are the worst of invasive species, and the best we could do would be to stop reproducing. Meanwhile, the college students are buckling themselves in to navigate the dystopian future. It's okay, they say. They are used to bad news: coronavirus canceled their graduation and flatlined their job prospects. Though they are at different stages right now, they all belong to Generation Z—from the kids in middle school to the young adults in college, serving in the armed forces, entering the working world, and starting to raise their own families.

Climate change is creating a spiritual emergency that hits Generation Z harder than any other generation. They can imagine living to 2060 or 2080 but only in a purely theoretical sense; they cannot actually envision what human life will be like then. Meanwhile, the lack of response to the climate crisis from the older generations creates a crisis of betrayal: realizing the adults in your life do not care about your future enough to change their ways. Thus young people need to become the adults they wish for and take on a terrifying amount of responsibility. Coming of age during the climate emergency is like learning to swim during a flood.

When Jesus put a child in the center and told the adults "be like this child, or you won't know heaven," he was not talking about childhood innocence (a concept that arrived on scene about seventeen centuries later). Perhaps it was simplicity he was talking about, or curiosity; he frequently called his disciples "children" or "little ones," with reminders that they were still learning and growing. Or perhaps, and even more likely, what he was talking about was the children's vulnerability. Their lives were unsure. In those days and in that kind of agrarian economy, children were seen less as precious treasures and more as uncertain investments. Beloved, still, yes, but quite vulnerable. Child mortality rates were grievously high. Coming "of age" was a big celebration, because it was not taken for granted. In this way, the young people of ancient times were quite like the young people of today: they faced uncertain futures. Millennia removed, Jesus's call to care for them, put them in the center, and pay attention to them rings true and clear in our context.

This book will help you keep young people in the center and listen to the troubles they have to share. Whether you are a Generation Z peer or a caring adult of any other generation, you will learn how to offer ecologically informed spiritual care.

Part One

JUMPING IN

For me as a person, I'm pretty cynical, so basically community is just what keeps me going. Because it's like, dang, if that person can do it, then I should probably be doing it, because it's better than just being hopeless about everything.

—MIMI, eighteen

We stood on the dock at Lake Tahoe staring at the water below: beautiful, crystal clear, and treacherously cold. Our church was on retreat here, and the eighth-grade boys insisted on tradition: the annual polar bear swim.

Some people think of polar bear swimming as winter swimming. At Lake Tahoe, which is deeper than the Empire State Building is tall and high enough in elevation that it is fed by melting snow year-round, most summer swims still qualify as polar bear swims. We have heard it rumored that if you come back at the very end of August and swim at high noon, you can manage to stay in for a few minutes without feeling the desperate need to quickly grow a few layers of blubber and fur. But it was an early June evening, and we who were not bears would be chilled to the bone.

Dean looked around and counted. Six of us.

"Wasn't William going to come too?" he asked, a little bit nervously.

"I think he said nah," Fred said, nonchalant as he shrugged off his shirt. Fred has Canadian blood and couldn't care less about the chill in the air.

"If he is coming, he had better hurry up and get here soon," Justine said, "because it's just getting colder." The sun had dropped low between the pines. Justine and her sister Norah were not wearing bathing suits—in fact, they were wrapped up in sweatshirts already—but they were there as witnesses and for a photo op as the sun went down. This would be their last retreat before college, so they would not miss out on documenting any important traditional moments.

My husband, Michael, dipped a toe in the water and hooted with gleeful anticipation. He dearly loves swimming, and when it comes to a dare, he is still an eighth-grade boy at heart.

I put a toe in too and pulled it back quickly, hopping around to try to stave off the cold. "Ooh, rookie mistake, Talitha," Norah said. "Now you've literally got cold feet and you aren't going to want to go in." When I baptized her in this lake three years ago (thankfully, on a very sunny afternoon), she did not let me waste time with toe dipping before we walked in.

"I didn't want to go in anyway," I said. "I can't believe I'm doing this."

"Yay! I see William!" Dean pointed out a figure on the shore, headed toward the dock.

"And Mimi. And Ray. And Easy?" Justine squinted to see who was in the rest of the approaching group. Two high school juniors and a ten-year-old.

"Whoa, even Ben is coming," Michael said, spotting our senior pastor with his kids. "I didn't know he was a polar bear too." Ben was clearly carrying a towel, though.

"Nellie too!" Fred hopped on top of the dock's rail. I assumed this was so he could see farther, even though he is incredibly tall already. But no, the rail was for another reason. "Okay, everyone get ready. Up on the rail!"

Dean clambered up with all the ease of an eighth-grade mountain goat. Michael hoisted himself up and looked down at me.

"*On* the rail?" I asked, backing away.

"It's tradition!" Fred bellowed, towering over us all.

William and his sister Mimi ran enthusiastically down the dock and hopped up on the rail. I actually had not known that we were all doing a high dive. I had prepped myself for a simple low jump off the bottom of the dock, more of a slide into the water, in and out again before my breath would be taken away. Apparently "tradition" had changed without notifying me. That's what you get when the eighth graders are in charge.

"I'm just holding the towels," Nellie announced as she arrived. Someone must have looked at her with a little too much expectation. Norah and Justine likewise held their arms out helpfully as the rest of the swimmers trooped over and hopped up.

Within a minute I was the last swimmer left standing on the dock. The moment of truth had arrived. The towel holders had their cameras ready.

"I would never, ever, ever in a million years be doing this if not for all of you," I grumbled as I clambered up between Fred and Michael. It was far too high for my comfort.

"Okay, everyone! Are you ready?" Dean spoke clearly and decisively, the young ringmaster of this group bonding exercise. "We're going to count down from five!"

"*Five*," Fred started the count.

"*Four*," everyone joined in.

"*Three*." I squirmed in agony, trying not to look down at the terrible distance between me and the water.

"Have courage, Talitha," Justine quipped from below, quoting back a line of the benediction I always use.

"*Two*—here we go!" Fred roared, and the shout of "*One!*" blended into screams of glee and terror. I reached for Michael's hand and felt the rush of bravery from all the shrieking enthusiasm around me and my feet moved of their own accord and I stepped out into nothing and fell.

Spending time with the youth makes me more courageous. I do things with them I would never do alone. And one of the most important things we can learn to do is to jump in together. We jump into the lake together as we jump into life together, as we commit together to the spiritual work before us, and as we engage in ecological work, scary though it may be. You cannot do the work of this life without jumping in and getting wet.

I would never do a polar bear swim of my own accord. Even my nearly aquatic husband can only rarely convince me to jump in with him. But surrounded by these shrieking teenagers, somehow, miraculously, I took the plunge.

You may find yourself teetering on the edge of ecological work, staring down at the painful reality below, discerning and deciding whether to dive in: whether to major in ecological studies, perhaps, or go vegan, or skip work or school for a protest, or take a stand at your city's town hall. You may find yourself stepping back, stepping forward, contemplating the high dive, looking away, and looking back again. It helps to be in the company of other jumpers and to have witnesses behind you. But there is no way to start, other than to start.

Stunned from the plunge, I swam up and surfaced gasping into a churning celebration. Yes, indeed, we had really done it. We swam around to the lower side of the dock, bumping into one another in our frenzied crawl, pastors and children and teenagers alike hooting and splashing and taking the Lord's name in vain. The world around us glowed with divine benevolence as the sunset deepened above us and around us in its reflection on the water. We hoisted ourselves onto the dock, and all the tension our bodies carried was left behind, floating down to the bottom of the lake. The towel-holding crew shone like saints as they distributed the blessed towels. Our teeth chattered and our skin rose in goose bumps as we swore that we would never do this again and that we would do it again tomorrow.

Chapter 1

All This Pain

How do you survive with all this pain in your heart?
Sometimes it feels like I cannot take any more.

—LUCIE, twenty-one

It was the summer of 2019, and our church had decided to send the youth on an ecological mission trip to the Pacific Ocean. We were driving down from Oakland to Monterey on an early Sunday morning in July. We got an early start, aiming to arrive before the host church's service, which means that it was still well before the ideal waking time of your average teenager. Most of them had shown up at our home church sleepyheaded, stuffed their bags in the back of the station wagon, plopped in their seats, pulled up their hoodies, inserted their earbuds, and promptly fallen asleep. So as I drove down the Oakland hills and toward the chilly fog of Monterey I was accompanied by three sleeping youth in my car, quiet and still. During this silent drive, God came at me to pry my heart open.

I knew something was up because I did not quite feel right. Usually I start a mission trip with a thrill and a kind of spiritual hunger. Mission trips are full of new tastes, thoughts, and experiences, and it is not only the youth who get excited; usually I am salivating at the adventures and opportunities before us. But that day as I drove, I was not spiritually hungry at all. I had a spiritual stomachache. I felt sour and off-balance inside. I was closed off, pulled in, locked up tight like a clam. I was scared. Scared? I had no reason to be scared. It was my sixth mission trip in six years, and none of them had been disasters so far.

It was not that I was afraid of the stress or the travel. The drive from Oakland to Monterey, with no traffic on a Sunday morning, is an easy two-hour journey. The road is beautiful and gentle: through the suburbs, past San Jose, into rolling hills, and then out down along the foggy shore. This was no high dive, as mission trips went; it was an easy slide into familiar waters. I should have been excited, not scared.

Even the work was going to be easy that week. On past mission trips, we have done some heavy lifting. We have burned our fingers in soup kitchens across several states; we have done lots of community gardening, including mowing and tilling; and we have wielded our share of power tools. But this year's trip was an ecological trip—a mission trip to the Pacific Ocean itself. The labor was quite different. Our hardest work would be picking up trash on beaches, and doing scientific surveys of the health of the local sand crab populations. We would be learning more than laboring; we would spend a whole day at the aquarium. I told myself that I should not be afraid, but inside I was barricaded and braced against my fear. And it would be a hard fear to address, because it was not logistical at all.

I realized what I was afraid of: I was afraid that I would fall in love.

I was afraid to fall in love with something fragile and vulnerable, something in mortal peril—that is, to fall in love with the ocean and its creatures. Ecological work is a difficult undertaking in this age of climate change, where species extinctions loom on every side. As the seas warm and rise, their creatures suffer. I knew that the youth in my car had boundless compassion for the creatures' suffering; I would be plunging in with them whether I liked it or not. Ecological work is more important than ever, but it runs the sharp risk of heartbreak as you stand there on the shore, throwing starfish after starfish back into a warming ocean. I was afraid my heart might break open with compassion for the plight of some struggling sea creatures and that it would be too painful to bear.

As I navigated around San Jose to Route 101, heart locked up tight, I assessed the risks. Whales? Sea lions? Sand crabs? My greatest risk would probably be otters. They are super endangered and problematically cute. You would think God had designed them to emotionally manipulate us into caring for them, with their adorable little faces. They even play with toys! I did not want to start caring about them.

My four-year-old nephew Tom had visited us for a few nights earlier that spring, toting a stuffed otter named George in his overnight bag and holding forth with all he knew about otters, which was a surprising amount for a four-year-old:

otters eat sea urchins, and sea urchins eat kelp, which means the otters ultimately help the kelp. Additionally, otters hold hands to stay together when floating, and they like to cuddle (particularly this one stuffed animal, who spent every night in Tom's bed). George was a cute toy. We got along fine. I knew the toys were designed to get kids to care about endangered species, but I did not really want to meet a real otter face-to-face and break the mental barrier between a sweet toy story to an animal in need. Something in me knew that if I started caring about the plight of the otters, I would never be able to stop. So I would just cut it off at the pass and call it a day. Slam down a wall in my heart. No new favorites for me.

Even as I thought these things I knew how funny they would sound if I were to say them aloud. Who wants to avoid love? Run away from caring? Avoid eye contact with one of the cutest creatures on the planet? But weird as the feeling was, it was also familiar. I had been here before. I felt this way as a college student in Europe. I was studying abroad in Prague, which is a lovely central spot from which a handful of college students might easily visit many other cities and countries; and indeed we did. But midway through the semester, I started dreading our weekend adventures. The weight of nostalgia was pulling me down. I already missed the town I had visited last weekend, and my photo album was thick with photographic adoration of cities and castles and gardens. How could I go on another trip? How could I add another place to love?

And I remember feeling this way the night before my first date with Michael, now my husband. I cried myself to sleep that night; I remember how badly I did not want to go on that first date. I had already met him and knew I liked him. But could I really open my heart to one more human being? I had already loved and lost—my ex-boyfriend had died in a tragic work accident—and I did not trust the sentimentalists who assured me 'twas better. Was it really? Grief hurts. Sometimes it incapacitates. It changes you. Did I really have the strength to open my heart up again?

Tom once said, with all his four-year-old wisdom, "There are so many people in the world that I love, and I wish we could all live together in one big house." That was the pain I was braced against. All the rooms in my heart were full. I already had my moment with great blue herons as a camp counselor fifteen years ago, and they still held a heavy nostalgic weight in my heart. I have always cared about the plight of the world's frogs, because I had a pet frog as a kid. And yes, we can take a moment to recognize that this was a weird choice of pets, but there is not a wide range of suitable pets for a big family living in a tiny New York City apartment. Frogs could fit.

And so as an adult, my heart is full of favorite creatures. I cannot fit another in my heart, and especially not an endangered one like the otters. I do not have room. I do not want to do it. Opening your heart up to ecological work during a climate emergency is like deciding to fall in love with a person who might be terminally ill. It is like deciding to walk into a hurricane: you don't do it on purpose.

As I crested the hills coming down toward Monterey, the ocean glimmered before me. There was not much longer to the drive; I knew I was going to have to settle this spiritual stomachache as best as I could before we got there and the youth all woke up, looking to me for inspiration and spiritual leadership. I took a breath and silently conjured up all the deep thoughts I could. From books, from poems, from seminary classes . . . from my own sermons, come back to preach at me in this hour of need. They rolled slowly, coming and going like waves, as the shell of my heart peeped open a crack and finally allowed God's spirit to flow inside.

God is love.
Love is of God.
Grief is the price of love.
God created us fragile, perishable.
God created the world fragile and perishable too.
God loves the world.
God loves fragile and perishable things.
God must be vulnerable to grief too.
Vulnerability is part of love.
This pain, then, that I feel, is God's spirit of love
    in me.
God aches for and loves the creatures in their peril.
It is our holy work to care for the fragile creatures
    and ecosystems that God so loves.
It is a holy thing to love what death can touch.

By the time we rolled through Monterey and around the bay to the exquisitely adorable town of Pacific Grove, where we would be staying at the Disciples of Christ church, my thoughts had settled down quietly. I can do this, I said to myself. I can jump in with the youth. It is just like the rest of life—the pain, the breaking, the opening, the growing. I can manage it. I can keep my heart open to love and grief and vulnerability and pain.

But so help me God, I still reserve the right to avoid eye contact with otters.

Chapter 2

I'm Not Okay, but I'm Okay

Look, the world
is always ending
somewhere.

—JAN RICHARDSON, "Blessing When the
World Is Ending" (excerpt)[1]

When I was in high school I befriended a girl about a year
younger than me, wild and impressionable, whose Russian
mother had named her Maria but who called herself Vivienne
because it was more sophisticated. She and her hardworking
mother were a small family in a small New York City apartment, and whatever her mother did, Vivienne wanted to do
differently. She didn't want to be successful or practical; she
wanted to be sophisticated, creative, spiritual, deep. She was

---

1   "Blessing When the World Is Ending" (excerpt) © Jan Richardson
    from *Circle of Grace: A Book of Blessings for the Seasons* (n.p.: Wanton
    Gospeller Press, 2015). Used by permission. janrichardson.com.

already well on her way to her goal of speaking seven languages. I had no new languages to share with her, but despite my poverty in languages, I did have a world to share with her: religion.

In her adolescent quest for a life different from her atheist mother's, Vivienne started tagging along to church with me. Sometimes she would sleep over on Saturday night and come with me in the morning; more surprisingly, some Sunday mornings she'd take a bus across upper Manhattan to arrive at Broadway Presbyterian Church in time for Bible study before the service. It was totally new to her, but she loved it.

After a few months, Vivienne told me that church had changed her perspective on life. I asked her what it was, assuming she had received some blessing of hope or grace. No, she said, what changed was that she had not realized before how many people were sick. She and her mother were healthy, and she didn't have anyone to lift up in prayer, but it seemed that every other person in the congregation was always lifting up a prayer for someone with cancer, with heart disease, with AIDS, with six months to live, with less. So many beloved people were in those terrible places where it felt like the world was ending.

I loved my church. I was rather obsessed with it. I was unbelievably grateful to have a chance to show my congregation off to a friend who was not bored by it. But at the same time, I had no idea what the real treasure on display was. I was into the organ music, the Taizé chants, our fun drama team, and the Bible studies where my youthful insights were as valued as any adult's. But Vivienne, though appreciating all these with enthusiasm, saw straight through to the even deeper heart of it. The thing here that could change your life, she saw, is the way people can show their vulnerability. The desperate prayer, the cry for help. That is the treasure, the rare shining glimpse of truth, in a world where everyone is so eager to show off their successes and strengths. That is the prize: to have your heart open in the place where the world is ending. Because it is always ending somewhere.

Opening our hearts to those who are suffering in those world-ending places is spiritual work. It is the plunge into shocking waters, the decision to dive in and care. It was life changing for Vivienne. We may be afraid of the pain; the fear of being overwhelmed by so much suffering is real. But the fragile, tender prize, that vulnerability that makes all life seem beautifully precious, is real too.

It is good and holy work to stay close to the places where the world is ending. It is important to participate in the litanies of lament, and remember how many people are suffering right now in floods and fires. It is a sacred task to name the people who have died, and to name the nonhuman species that are at the end of their own particular world, and to mark their passing as they move into extinction.

If we stray too far from the ending edge of the world, we may locate the apocalypse entirely in the future. This kind of environmentalism is a familiar caricature: people get in a tizzy about potential suffering in the future, mourning dramatically over the fact that their hypothetical grandchildren may not ever get to see real elephants, or polar bears, or tigers—not even in zoos. But meanwhile, they are oblivious to the suffering their human and nonhuman neighbors are experiencing right now.

Don't fool yourself with worrying about how the apocalypse is coming. It is here. Somewhere the world has ended with a million-acre fire. Here it has ended with a rising sea level; there, with a long, slow drought. Somewhere close to you it has ended with Covid-19 sweeping through a nursing home . . . or a prison.

And the suffering of the nonhuman creatures is not in the future either. The fog near Santa Cruz is poisoned with mercury, and the mountain lions are suffering. The starfish off Mendocino are all dying of some mysterious wasting disease. Ecosystems and habitats are disappearing now, leaving creatures homeless and hungry. The world is on fire *now*, and the burning hurts.

We learn how to be emotionally present to the enormity of ecological suffering in much the same way we learn to have our hearts open to the suffering of other people. Just like Vivienne did, we go to church and participate in the long litanies of who is sick, who is near death, who has died. We pray for the people lifted up in prayer even if we do not know them, trying to imagine what it must be like for them, asking God's mercy, sending our love. We attend funerals in our community even when we did not know the deceased well; we just show up to bear witness to their life. This builds our spiritual resilience as we widen our capacity to hold the suffering of others in mind. When people are killed in tragic ways, whether near or far, we participate in the vigils and protests. Praying for them may mean reading the names of those dead of Covid-19 or carrying signs with the names of those who have been killed by the police. Prayer is an act of attention, and being attentive to those who are suffering leads us to open our hearts to them.

And we learn in action, by showing up with help for those who are suffering. We open our hearts in tangible ways when we do acts of service for one another. When my mother went through chemo, her next-door neighbor took her neighborliness up a few notches and cooked for my parents. Every Monday, she would bring dinner. She kept it up for months, until my mother's stamina and appetite had returned fully. I learned a lot from that. Simple, consistent, generous acts of love go a long way when things are tough.

Midway between the communal prayer litanies and the hands-on helping, we find the ministry of presence. This involves showing up for someone with nothing or not much in your hands; you are just there to witness and support. This can be the hardest. If only you had a casserole or something helpful in your hands, it might be easier, but there are things that a casserole cannot help. Sometimes you show up without even a sympathy card. Sometimes you get a text message and head straight to the hospital waiting room, empty handed.

In fall 2017, the smoke from the Santa Rosa fires blew down on a hot wind into the hills of Oakland, toxic and stinking. This was still a rare experience that year, and most of us did not have respirator masks or air filters yet. We were well equipped with caution and fear, however; our neighborhood was the site of the tragic 1991 firestorm that killed twenty-five people, destroyed more than three thousand homes, and caused an estimated $1.5 billion of property loss. Those were not just figures to the members of Montclair Presbyterian Church; they were vivid memories. Many church members were among the victims, and everyone remembers the weeks after the fire, when the church fellowship hall became an emergency supply station. So in 2017, when the smoke blew down into our neighborhoods and the TV filled with images of devastation from the North Bay, our community hunkered down, anxious and afraid.

Lacking the filters and masks that would become a major part of our lives in the coming years, we just had to cope with the choking smoke as well as we could. Most of us sealed off our windows with tape, stayed inside, and felt sick. Melyssa felt sick like the rest of us, coughing and queasy, but then she got sicker . . . and sicker. And then suddenly she was unable to get up one morning, and her mom called an ambulance, which took her to the hospital, to the ICU, in a coma.

Melyssa is a beloved young adult in our community, one of the older of the Generation Z crowd. She is incredibly friendly; she joined the church years ago, after she met a bunch of teens from our church in a line to see a movie together. By the end of that night, they were all fast friends, and a few months later she went on her first youth group retreat with them. As soon as she graduated high school, she became a junior advisor for the youth group and became a full-fledged chaperone as soon as she was allowed by the safety policy. She is a "little person," a dwarf, about the same height as some of the bigger children she supervises in the church nursery. My two-year-old niece fell immediately in love with her and wanted to call her on the phone after church. The youth group members value her as a confidante and friend; she counsels them through the deepest of dramas and helps them breathe through their worst panic attacks. She searches out and seeks the lost, whether that is a teen hiding moodily behind a phone or a child too shy to take part in the Christmas pageant. The entire church community, of every generation, was devastated to hear the news of her illness.

Her mother kept vigil at the side of her bed in the ICU and told me, "Talitha, I just don't know what I would do if I lost her." It would be the end of the world for her if that happened; Melyssa, her only child, is everything to her. Doctors came in and shared their latest theories—perhaps the wildfire smoke had triggered some major reaction, or perhaps the smoke irritation symptoms had been masking some other trouble—but nobody really knew why this was happening or how to fix it or whether she would ever wake up again. Church people stopped by the hospital as often as we could over the coming weeks. We could not do anything either—at least nothing that mattered. We could bring her mom a meal or offer a ride home to get clean laundry, but we could not wake Melyssa up.

It is so hard to show up helpless. There is no doubt that it would be easier to stay home. But the cost of staying home is too often a closed-off heart, which stands in the way of our spiritual growth. At those terrible places—the end of one world or another or the almost-ending places—we need to open our hearts and not turn away. We need to jump in.

It would be dishonest to skip straight to how Melyssa made a great recovery. She did make a great recovery! But before that, she fought for her life. When she woke up it was discovered that she had a serious undiagnosed medical condition that had been exacerbated by the smoke and stress. She went through some complicated surgeries, and she learned to live with an arsenal of medications and their side effects. And we who watched, visited, and prayed learned from her. She did not take life for granted anymore. Living, breathing, eating, and having the strength to take a walk around the block . . . and after a while to show up at church, play games with the youth . . . these all shone with the glow of Melyssa's gratitude, because she knew that none of them was guaranteed.

Do not remember the former things,
    or consider the things of old.
I am about to do a new thing;
    now it springs forth, do you not perceive it?
I will make a way in the wilderness
    and rivers in the desert.

                      —Isaiah 43:18–19

I remember the first time I felt like I came near to the end of the world. Looking back on it, I see how minor it really was, but at the time, I had no such perspective. I was studying at the State University of New York, and the school faced drastic budget cuts. I was majoring in music, and many of my classes and all of my ensembles were deemed inessential and were destined for the chopping block. The degree I hoped to finish might not be available after all.

"What on earth am I going to do?" I sighed to my parents, sitting around their wooden dining room table in their apartment in Manhattan. "I can't start all over again!"

"It's okay, it's okay," they hushed.

"You won't have to start from scratch. You can do another major," my dad said, perhaps hoping that this time he would convince me to study philosophy.

"Or if you really want to do music, then choose any other school," my minister mom said, plain and simple. "You'll get transfer credits. You could find another good fit."

"It's just so awful, though," I lamented. "We have such a great jazz band. They're just going to let it go."

"Hey, hey, calm down," my dad said. "It's not the end of the world."

I rankled at this. I may have been obsessed, but jazz band was actually most of my little world: it included the majority of my friends and took up many of my leisure hours as well.

"It *is* the end of the world to me!" I wailed, slamming my open hands down on the wooden table so hard the spoons jumped.

"Okay," he muttered humbly. "Maybe it is. Maybe it is."

I let out my pent-up breath, finally feeling heard.

But he couldn't resist having the last word. It came from deep in his Buddhist-Christian core.

"But," he said—and I glared a little—"but there will be a new heaven and a new earth." My mom smiled faithfully, her hope unshaken by my angsty earthquake.

I grudged Dad the last word and left the table silently. I was not yet ready for his hopeful salve on my raw wounds, but the next day on the bus back to college I wrote it down in my journal. "All things have to die and be mourned for," I wrote in purple marker jostled from the road, "and even if this is the end there will be a beginning."

I went back to school, loving my jazz band even more deeply as I made myself open my eyes to the possibility it could be our last performance. By the time we finished the semester the financial tides had turned somehow, and it was announced that our program would continue. I remember my saxophonist friend lifted his head and screamed when I told him the joyful news.

So with reverence for all that this almost-world-ending moment taught me, I am flatly in awe at the sheer amount of such spiritual work the young people have had to do today. Many of them had their particular world ended or threatened by firestorm or flood or drought, but even those who were not victims of "natural" disasters still dealt with something. Coronavirus ripped them all untimely from their jazz bands, their a cappella groups, and their science fair projects; everything got canceled. Life demanded of them at virus-point that they learn quickly how to love and let go, to detach, to separate, to untangle the threads of longing and planning. They had to learn to be "okay" at those edges of the ending world. They had to learn to detach from their expectations without actually detaching from the world; to love the world as they know it and grieve and let it go at the same time.

Eighteen-year-old Ray displayed an impressive amount of equanimity as their world ended in March 2020. They missed their high school prom and their last youth group mission trip; graduation turned into a semiprivate drive-through ceremony and all the parties were canceled. Would they get to go to college, out of state, as planned? They shrugged, ready for whatever came. I was in awe of Ray's equanimity, given the whiplash of these cancelations. Perhaps it was their experience in the local youth circus that kept them balanced—they were, after all, quite comfortable juggling whatever their friends threw at them. I had to ask where this magic was coming from.

Sitting on the sidewalk outside our church, six feet apart and wearing masks, together Ray and I chalked "Black Lives Matter" in big letters. It felt like a good activity for a Monday afternoon in June 2020, something meaningful to do for those of us who were crying out inside to respond to the latest round of police brutality but whose family members did not want us downtown facing still-unknown risks of exposure to coronavirus at the newly erupting protests. We knew that it was also important to carry the message to our wealthy and predominantly white neighborhood, with its legacy of being a refuge for the privileged; we knew it was likely some people would drive by and give us the finger. But we also had families coming by, appreciating the message, joining our work, and bringing extra chalk supplies. It is a long sidewalk, so we had lots of time to talk as we chalked. Ray stretched out, nearly in a split, chalking the letters in strong outlines for me to color in.

"How are you doing?" I asked them, not the most graceful phrase to use during such a time of crisis.

"Eh," Ray said, "you know. I'm not okay, but I'm okay."

"Well said," I responded, wondering what made the difference.

"At least I'm older now," they said, "and I can do something. I can vote, I can protest." November 2020 would be their first election, just five months away now.

"What a time to cast your first ballot." And I thought but did not say out loud, *What a time to hit the streets protesting for the first time, with all this pent-up energy and yet unsure what is safe.*

"Yeah, it's something. I mean, it helps me feel better. I feel bad for the younger people who have to just watch it happen. Even if my vote doesn't make that much of a difference, still it feels good to be able to do something. And I have my license now; I can drive here and do this. I feel like if I were younger, I would be so paralyzed."

As I picked up another piece of chalk, it struck me that I was not nearly grateful enough for the privileges of adulthood that Ray so relished: a voter registration card and driver's license. These are the markers and gifts of coming-of-age, which for Ray functioned as a kind of fulcrum to push them out of paralysis and into action, however small. The ability to drive themself to the church was enough for today. The ability to chalk the sidewalk instead of doing nothing would do, for now. Because the alternative—sitting at home, isolated from the pain of the world—would feel wrong.

But I had forgotten to be grateful for these gifts. For having the keys to my own car and not even needing to consult a family member for permission to take it for a drive. Like the gift of health, taken for granted so often prepandemic, or the gift of fresh air, appreciated much more keenly after last autumn's brutal wildfire season. We had not known about being grateful for fresh air back then. Remember when we did not have to wear masks? Remember way back when we did not even *have* face masks? We now have wardrobes of masks for all varieties of disaster preparedness. We are learning, slowly, to be grateful for the things we once took for granted.

The world is always ending somewhere. Somewhere with a virus, somewhere with a budget cut, somewhere with a million-acre fire, and somewhere with police brutality. Even when we feel empty-handed and useless, it is spiritually important for us to open up to the pain. So instead of staying at home, we drive to the church and hold vigil as we chalk the heartbreaking names up and down the street: George Floyd. Breonna Taylor. Sandra Bland.

Now some endings turn into beautiful new beginnings, like Melyssa swinging back into church activities or like my jazz band's joy when we lived to play another year. In these cases, we will be grateful and glad that we jumped in with hearts open, because if we had closed off, we would have missed the beauty of beginning again. Other endings are simply endings;

there is no beginning again for Breonna Taylor. Still, we turn toward the endings with grief, compassion, and awe. And we hold on to that faith in a new heaven and a new earth. We hold on to the promise of new life, and the abundance that is constantly springing up around us. A wave crashes on the beach and it is no more, but the energy of that wave is still held and kept in the vastness of the ocean. All things must die and be mourned for, but none are ever lost from God's eternal hands.

Chapter 3

Together, We Can Make It

Community is a big part of making change in the
world and giving each other hope.

—JUSTINE, nineteen

Our church leadership team was on retreat in the redwoods.
We started our meeting on a beautiful foggy morning. We
sang, prayed, did an icebreaker or two. Later in the morning,
we chatted pleasantly about welcoming people to church.
Sunday school teachers, youth group advisors, board members, and committee chairs all shared their ideas for welcoming people. We could offer welcome packets to newbies. We
could explain more clearly our tradition of offering white and
red ceramic cups at the coffee hour; how you are supposed
to pick a red cup if you are new so that old-timers know to
approach you and be friendly. We could designate prechurch
and postchurch greeters. "What about if we used special colored nametags?" someone asked. It was all a light conversation
until Jim dared to speak. Jim is a halfway-retired therapist and

lay pastor who has volunteered in just about every corner of the church. He is popular with the eighth-grade boys in youth group for his dry humor and easygoing manner. Usually, he speaks up to crack a joke. But this time he spoke slowly and softly, bringing the sparkling lilt of our casual conversation down to a slow rolling thunder.

"I don't think the cups and nametags and stuff make a difference. People who walk through the doors of the church aren't looking for 'a nice experience'—if they wanted that, they'd go to a concert in the park. If you're like me, the first couple of times you visit a church, you're coming because you're in spiritual need. You come with a deep problem you can't even talk about, but it forces you to seek help, and you think church might be the only place to find it. It doesn't matter if we give them a cute brochure if we can't minister to them in their need."

A sacred silence surrounded his words as everyone took them in. He spoke about his own spiritual crisis, wrestling with real problems and feeling "not good enough" in every aspect of his life. He did not come to church because it was a nice place to get involved; he came because he was spiritually starving. He recognized he could not meet his own spiritual needs on his own.

When he was done talking the silence was rich in the room. People sighed and settled more deeply into their chairs. The moderator thanked him slowly and carefully. And then one of those blessed logistics-minded people—you know them, the people with checklists—enthusiastically blurted out, "Let's do it! So how do we meet people's spiritual needs?"

How indeed.

Meeting people's spiritual needs is a sacred and often-ineffable task, much harder than providing a special cup or nametag for visitors. It often requires us to dive with them into the depths of suffering, longing, and brokenness. And the task is shrouded in mystery, too; we do not always know that we have met someone's spiritual needs until perhaps later, when they thank us for something that turned out to be very important to them. There is no simple how-to guide that takes away the depth of this work. But nonetheless, it can be learned, by anyone who wants to try.

When we think of providing spiritual support to young people in crisis, we might get hung up on the idea that we should provide advice or lessons, that somehow we should have spiritual treasures to give or at least a treasure map. But the beautiful and liberating truth is that each person will figure out what to do and does not need you to give them a road map. They only need to be accompanied as they work things out in their own souls with God. They do not need someone standing in the water telling them how and where to jump in; they need someone at their side ready to jump with them.

My husband, Michael, is a professional trainer; he teaches the city employees in San Francisco, thousands of employees, with new ones coming in each month. He gives a variety of classes, from orientation up through diversity and antiracism classes. It is a cool job, very cool indeed, and before he worked there, I really did not understand that this kind of job existed. Years ago he told me his dream job was to be a trainer, and I looked at him as if he had decided to be a kangaroo. I was skeptical because I did not know about any professional trainers except for professors and other specialists who led trainings in their particular area of expertise, so I assumed he was a PhD or at least a few best-selling books away from becoming a real pro. But, no, there is a whole field called talent development, and you do not need to be a specialist in any subject to work in this field. What you need is good pedagogy—good teaching methods. And Michael has great pedagogy. He is great with a PowerPoint presentation, excellent at leading discussions, a masterful speaker, skilled at crafting the right listener-response question, and funny enough to keep people from falling asleep when the HR-mandated topic is less than riveting.

We also need good pedagogy in the spiritual life. We might assume that the only way to help people spiritually is to be spiritual giants ourselves: to pray for a few years in seclusion and come to incredible insights, to get that PhD and wear that mortarboard proclaiming *more spiritual than thou*, to be a specialist. That is the same mistake I made when I assumed Michael was not yet qualified to be a professional trainer.

But you are hereby released from the pressure of needing to be a spiritual giant, because you can help meet people's spiritual needs without much more than some good pedagogy. A few spiritual experiences of your own will help, yes, but it is amazing how much you can accomplish for others, not by sharing your own hard-won wisdom, but by just knowing the techniques to listen, resonate, and respond.

All of our spiritual needs are seriously affected by the climate crisis. The young people of Generation Z are coming of age in the chaos of fire and flood. They need ecologically attuned spiritual care.

Many people assume our spiritual needs will be met on the fly, with not much help from others—maybe especially here in California, where the spiritual-but-not-religious vibe lends itself easily to contemplative walks in the woods and "moments of quiet reflection" with no instruction needed. Perhaps these are the low-hanging fruit of spirituality; one does not need much instruction or support to engage in them. Guided meditation? Yeah, there's an app for that! In the privacy of your earbuds, you too can get spiritual, and you don't have to tell anyone about it. But sometimes a walk in the woods and a few minutes of quiet cannot address your spiritual needs. If you are in a major spiritual crisis because climate change has flooded your future, you may need something a little more robust than a few minutes of quiet. And not all communities—not even all religious communities—are prepared to provide the spiritual support you will need. Many churches tend to operate as if a person's involvement in the community will naturally progress from attending worship, to joining formally, to finally serving on a committee or even being nominated for council . . . all without much more spiritual support needed. You just join and get involved. Of course there is prayer involved, some words between you and God, but those depths are private!

Spiritual growth is indeed natural, God given, and organic. Each of us has a spiritual drive within, as tenacious as a dandelion that reaches for the sun even in neglected places like the crack between wall and pavement. But even as we appreciate how natural it is, we can also learn how to nurture it well. We can support one another with love, with guidance, and sometimes with confrontation. These are techniques we can learn and practice.

The garden in front of my house also grows organically and naturally, but that does not mean I do not take some time to read books, get ideas from fellow gardeners, and text my more experienced friends to ask for tips. Some may affirm they can grow spiritually anywhere—on a mountaintop, at dinner with friends, in a book at the library—and this is true. God is everywhere, your spirit is hungry, and the world is full of spiritual food. Yes! You can glean as you go and get your spiritual needs met on the fly. But do you not know that you can also cultivate spiritual growth deliberately? Do you not know that there are ways for us to get through this hard work together? And if you are starving because a fire or flood has come through town and ruined all your gardens and crops, it will be essential to have community support.

Looking at the climate emergency, we hear God's call: for those of us who have been blessed to have spiritual nourishment, it is time to dig deep and share those gifts. This is no time to keep your blessings to yourself. As the climate changes, we will get hungrier, body and soul. Those times when we did not need to attend to the hungers of our souls because they were fed au naturel from the fat and rich land around us will give way—yielding to times where we must carry bread for the journey, flat bread that tastes like the desert, with no time to allow the dough to rise. We have to learn how to live in the wilderness. Spiritually solo, we are not likely to survive long enough to see Generation Z through. But together, we can make it.

Chapter 4

Exercises in Vulnerability

I'm torn between wanting so much to fix everything but also feeling a pessimism that it's hopeless.

—LINNEA, twenty-two

To make it through the climate crisis (inasmuch as we can say
"through" knowing we will not see the end of it), we need to
build the capacity to do hard things. A lot of hard things are
coming up and the young people I know are all training to
deal with them in different ways. Ray is in college now and is
ready to do whatever it takes to become a lawyer and sue corporations on behalf of the earth. Linnea, just graduating from
college, is already hard at work managing wild ecosystems to
preserve biodiversity. Lily is raring to get into politics. All of
these tracks will take them down different roads, and there
will be huge challenges for each of them as they go: sacrifices,
selflessness, trauma, grief, and failure.

Whether we are their elders or peers, we who are part
of their spiritual ecosystems need to help them develop the

capacity to do hard things. How can we teach them to pick themselves up again when they stumble? When they go up against the powers that be, the powers that be will lash back against them, and their well-intentioned efforts will be slammed aside. They will see cities washed away and beloved creatures going extinct. And they will take their righteous anger to city hall or to the streets and see it fall flat. They will need support.

Whether their stumbling blocks are grief, anger, or despair (and there will be plenty of each to go around), the most important spiritual gift will be simply how to keep going.

We spend much of our lives pretending that things are not hard for us. Educational psychologists are uncovering the harsh legacy of this pretense, counting the cost when children learn to hide their struggles and only attempt tasks they are sure they can conquer. Many of us grew up being praised for our good results, not our hard work. We were praised when we breezed through something easy for us but not praised when we attempted something too hard for us and fell short. The harder task may have been much better for our growth and learning; nevertheless, we learned to try only easy things. That approach will not take us far in the worldwide fight to heal and cool our climate; if our eyes are too fixed on the prize of success, we will estimate the odds and decide not to try at all. We have to be willing to try something hard, heavy, and emotionally taxing with no guarantee of success at all. We need to develop a resilience deep enough to risk failure and keep going. We need the courage to jump into uncertain waters.

What is the hardest thing you have ever done? You can take this question any way you want; you can brag about your biggest accomplishment or mourn over the most emotionally taxing thing you have ever survived. What made it so hard? And why did you do it anyway? Sometimes we rise to meet challenges, and sometimes we do not or cannot. What makes the difference? What pushes you from "I can't" to "I can"?

Most of my stories about the "hardest thing I've ever done" took place during my hospital chaplaincy residency. I signed up for this residency as a stalling technique. I was done with grad school and ready to go anywhere, but I was dating this great guy and did not want to test our relationship geographically. I looked around for something nearby, and the idea of a yearlong residency seemed perfect.

There was one slight hitch: I hated hospitals.

I had been a hospital volunteer in high school, working two-hour shifts after school on a geriatric acute care unit with next to no supervision. Nurses would ask me to refill water pitchers (easy) or feed patients who needed help eating (I was shy but I managed) or to help them change postsurgical dressings (*What?* But I was too shy to say no, and I helped until the nurse noticed that my face was going pale and then green). I walked in on a dead person once; I was supposed to feed her dinner, but the nurse did not know she had died. The social worker discovered me standing there blankly and put me to work running paperwork through the copier, but she did not ask me how I was doing after having encountered death. I screwed up my courage and powered through.

After each shift, I had a few blocks to walk home, and during these walks, I was often filled with strange and urgent desires to dance, to eat an entire pizza, to run through the park, to fall down in a snowbank, to stand out in the rain, or at least to spend an hour in the shower. I did not know how to handle the hard things I had experienced. The idea of processing my difficult experiences by phoning a friend—or even telling a family member when they asked how my day was—did not cross my mind. The turmoil was *inside* me; I would have to shake it out somehow.

So when I signed up for my hospital chaplaincy residency, I assumed that I would be in a similar survival mode all year long. But I knew I would grow strong, like a warrior at spiritual boot camp. My shell would harden, like a soft little baby turtle growing into adulthood, and tough experiences would roll off me like water off a turtle's shell.

I was surprised to find that I actually loved it.

There was a lot to love from my point of view. I loved having a belt full of pagers showing how important I was. I loved tapping my badge—beep!—and getting immediate access to a room, a unit, or a computer where I would chart really fast, sitting with my back ramrod straight, looking around to see who might be impressed by my typing speed. Hospitals encourage and celebrate this kind of performative efficiency, and I like that dance.

But I ended up loving the work too. I met wonderful people, patients who were doing amazing spiritual work in their hospital beds, doing the "hardest thing you've ever done" of their lives right then and there as they recovered from surgeries or came to terms with diagnoses. And I had great colleagues, especially the therapists who roped me and my guitar in for group sing-alongs on the psych unit. But the best thing that happened to me that year was the work of integration. Over the year I learned to use my full self—not just my tough side—in service of this ministry. I learned to stop armoring up for the hard tasks. I learned to seek resilience instead of brute strength.

I had to do a really hard thing on my first on-call overnight shift. It was a Code White—a very sick child needing resuscitation. The pagers woke me at 3 a.m.; I jumped off my cot in the on-call room and rushed to the pediatric ICU. I tried to do my duty, standing near the parents and offering gentle emotional support while the doctors and nurses valiantly kept this child alive, but it was terrifying. They had a scope down into this child's lungs and they were sucking blood clots out. The scope image was projected on a computer screen for all to see. It was my first view into anyone's lungs, and these small lungs were filled with blood, barely hanging on to life. What's more, these troubled lungs were inside a beloved child, a small frail body, unconscious and intubated, with his parents weeping nearby. After a while, it was all so overwhelming that I had to leave and sit in the bathroom and put my head down until the blood stopped pounding in my ears. But I went back after the code ended and checked in with the family, because that was my job. As I left the family at the bedside, I felt like I had done a lousy job of it, leaving them in their moment of need.

I berated myself for my weakness as I fell back onto my cot to sleep restlessly. The next morning after I had handed over the pagers to the next chaplain, I talked to my supervisor, Peter. I wanted to know where I went wrong. I sat in his office, eagerly awaiting my boot-camp discipline. But Peter had nothing but compassion for me.

"Talitha, I think you did as well as you could in a hard situation."

I was not so sure about that. I asked what I could have done better. He sat back, cocked his head, and looked at me for a moment.

"What *could* you have done better?"

"I mean, it was just rough, I guess, but how should I have handled it?"

"There's nothing you did wrong," he said. "The only thing I can think of is that you could have called me."

"Right then, at 3 a.m.?"

"Yes, Talitha, because you were upset and *you* needed support."

"Oh." I think I kept my jaw from dropping, but internally I was astounded. With that one offer from Peter, I began unlearning the lessons I had given myself in that early, unsupervised, unsupported volunteer stint.

This was not going to be an exercise in muscling through and getting tough; this was going to be an exercise in vulnerability.

We can use lots of different tools to help us do hard things. As a chaplain, you rely on the tools in your hands: pager, clipboard, badge, perhaps some prayer books or poetry. But more than that, you must use your *self*, your full and rich self, including the soft and vulnerable underbelly, not just the sharp professional side. You cannot make it through the hard things without this vulnerability. You must dive into the depths of your grief, your own tears, your compassion, and your suffering. We cannot build resilience by toughening up and refusing to let the bad feelings inside; that is just a way of treading water. We get strong by going deep. We take our grief to our colleagues and mentors. We dive in, swim down, touch the terrible bottom, and swim up again.

When I first faced the spiritual work we all need to do to get through the climate crisis, my impulse was to imagine it as one big toughening-up exercise. As if we could do spiritual calisthenics, get spiritually strong, and by our strength guarantee that the pain and the grief would roll off our souls like water drops tumbling off a turtle's shell. We could watch another town burn, see another species brought to extinction, and instead of mourning, just move straight into action. We would go to jail for civil disobedience without batting an eye or needing to process the trauma. We would wear armor on our souls. Our strength would be limitless. We would have no needs. But this vision is ultimately a spiritual bypass—an impossible myth.

What we need, instead, are generous supporters, like my supervisor Peter, who will be glad to receive our 3 a.m. distress cries. We need to build our capacity to serve one another in this deep way—and deepen our capacity to jump into the vulnerable mess of it all. As adrienne maree brown writes, we need to focus less on "critical mass" in our activist work and more on "critical .connections." We need communities of shared intimacy, open hearts connected, who can support one another in conversation or in wordless presence. We need to share our ecological grief, our anger, our despair—and have it received. We need "check-in" times when we can safely fall apart for a while, held in love as we cry.

> *Giant Oak, in his strength & his scorn*
> *Of the winds, by the roots was uptorn:*
> *But slim Reeds at his side,*
> *The fierce gale did outride,*
> *Since, by bending the burden was borne.*
>
> —a fable of Aesop[1]

We must learn to experience our own vulnerability if we are to do the important work of supporting others in their vulnerability. As my chaplain residency supervisor, Peter accompanied me on patient visits every once in a while, watching and giving feedback. He came with me to see an anorexic patient, twenty-two years old and weighing all of sixty-four pounds. She was hospitalized against her will; she would have chosen to continue starving herself, even though it was already giving her seizures. Anorexia is a brutal illness and she was brutally ill, in body and mind. Visiting her would be hard

1 Walter Crane, *The Baby's Own Aesop: Being the Fables Condensed in Rhyme with Portable Morals Pictorially Pointed* (1887; New York: George Routledge & Sons, 1908), 24, accessed March 22, 2021, https://publicdomainreview.org/collection/the-baby-s-own-aesop-1908.

for me in particular; I find eating disorders especially disturbing because I have had several friends and family members who struggled with them. I had looked at this patient's chart several times that week and made one excuse or another to put her on the end of each day's list. Conveniently, I never got around to visiting her. With Peter next to me, though, I trusted I could do any hard thing, so we went to see her.

We introduced ourselves. She smiled politely. She did not engage. She sat there, confined to her bed, tightening and releasing her muscles in place without moving, which was the only allowed form of exercise (exercise being one of the addictions wrecking her small body). I tried to chat. I threw some feeling words out to see if she would engage sadness, anger, happiness, or fear. Most patients will latch on to one or another of these feelings like Velcro, but with her, it was like trying to get marbles to stick to a chalkboard. Every attempt rolled off her shell with a polite smile. She was one tough cookie. Her "sitter," an older physician's assistant in the chair next to her bed who was charged with watching to make sure she did not toss her cookies (in the trash *or* in the euphemistic sense), smiled grimly at me. She was watching for a twelve-hour shift; she had no illusions about how impossibly addicted this patient was to her disorder. I said goodbye, the patient chirped "Okay!" with the fakest of smiles, and we were out of there.

Afterward in the hallway, Peter debriefed me. But I felt utterly helpless. Nothing had stuck.

"You really wanted to help her." Peter's gaze was firm and kind.

"Yeah," I admitted. Perhaps more than my average patient. "I thought I could help." *Oh. I had my fix-it cape on, didn't I? I'm always tripping over that.*

"She didn't want help."

"Not a bit."

He sat and didn't say anything else. The plain facts hung in the air: I wanted to help her, but she would not or could not receive my help. I wanted to be her savior, or at least her hero. I did not want to be helpless.

Sometimes it is hard to admit that our best efforts have a really low chance of success. My best efforts were pretty useless that day; it would have been easier not to visit her at all.

Peter sat there, head cocked in curiosity as all this rolled through my mind. He asked, "So how did you feel, Talitha?"

Ah, there it was. A few miserable tears leaked out of my eyes. I took a tight breath.

"Sad," I squeaked out.

"Sad. Yes. It was sad, wasn't, it, to see her like that?"

I nodded, mute, and as the tears rolled I started to feel a little lighter in spirit.

Peter just sat there and kept me company as I cried. He did not have any further wisdom for me. He was just there to sit with me in my helplessness so I could let go of those tears. But it was more than enough; I was not alone.

We need complex metaphors to represent how helplessly sick our planet is with climate change. An addictive disease like anorexia just about fits. Eating disorders are progressive, difficult to treat, and sometimes fatal. They are diseases in one way and addictions in another. A powerful mix of therapies must come together just right before an eating disorder *can* be cured, from medical treatment and supervision, through all kinds of therapy, to healthy community support. Some cases cannot be cured, and we cannot always pinpoint why. Even if someone is able to change and heal for a while, they can be sucked back down as cruelly and arbitrarily as a cancer relapse. We do not know enough about how to cure them; we need more studies, more insight, and more treatment options. Our best efforts do not guarantee success.

The climate emergency is likewise caused by a complex of addictive behaviors and conditions. We are plainly hooked on fossil fuels; the effort needed to wrench ourselves free from our well-established systems of reliance is formidable. If we are to free and heal our climate, we need a lot of different kinds of "therapies." We need healthier alternatives; we need to invest in new infrastructure, new power plants, new and smarter electric grids. We need greener cities, not built around the needs of the automobile but built for lower-intensity ways of living. We need to strip away the political power held by fossil fuel companies and put people power to work for the health of the planet. We need political will, from international coalitions to community organizations. We need new technologies. And though they are statistically less important than the structural therapies, we also need a host of person-by-person commitments and sacrifices: eating less meat, forgoing flying, reducing food waste or waste in general, and getting off the plastic train. We are in deep, deep need. And our best efforts are certainly not guaranteed to succeed.

Addictions, from eating disorders to fossil fuels, usually come with protective circles around them. There are circles of denial, the thoughts and rationalizations that let us believe things are better than they are. They tell us, "It's okay to skip dinner now and then," ignoring the fact that it's been every night for a month. They tell us, "It's okay, climate change won't be as bad as the scientists say," ignoring the fact that it has already proved to be worse than initially predicted. We may be even more familiar with how denial functions around alcoholism. Denial keeps us from looking deep into the abyss and realizing how out of control we are. Denial tells us that we *are* in control, that we can stop whenever we want to, and that we will be sure to put on the brakes before we crash. But our reactions might not be quick enough, especially if we are driving up the wrong side of the highway and our senses are dulled by drink. And our world is surely in the wrong lane right now, hurtling toward disaster.

Generation Z stands back and watches the older generations drunk driving down the road of ecological denial with the kind of dumbfounded stare you might get from a kid asked to believe that it is really okay if Uncle Jake is "just like that when he drinks." They are not ready to take up that mantle of protective denial we would pass down to them.

We build protective circles around our addiction-disease complexes. Habits of behavior keep things as they are. Because of these encircling habits, if you want to unhook from an addiction, everything around it will probably need to be changed too. You know, the little things that kept our unhealthy lives in balance. Maybe someone used to need a few cocktails to unwind after a hard day at work. It was just part of the routine. Well, now that they are "on the wagon," they may need to find a new way to deal with the fact that 9-to-5 capitalism is actually deadening their soul. Maybe adding a kickboxing class will do? Or maybe they will need to find a new job. Likewise with the climate crisis, perhaps we used to take vacations to distant and beautiful places to unwind after a hard season, but if we wean ourselves off the jet fuel bottle, we are going to need to find new ways to cope with the fact that our rat-race lives and ugly neighborhoods are dragging us down.

In any addiction, circles of people are willing to help us stay addicted. They will enable and protect our destructive behaviors, either because they benefit from them directly (our drug dealers and our fossil fuel companies) or because the work required for our healing would be "too much" (those who believe the status quo will keep them safer than radical change). They keep the liquor cabinet well stocked and the price of gas low. They whisper reassurances when we worry that perhaps someone has lost too much weight, repeating the accepted party line that you can never be too rich or too thin. They sweep an oil spill under the rug and throw away the article about the fires in Australia before the kids see it. They ask the church to please feed the homeless people at the back door so we do not have to see them on our morning walk. Thus they maintain the illusion of things being okay.

Some people would not want to enable the addiction in such a direct way, but they may be in such desperate straits that they would lash out if we tried to change anything. Perhaps their lives are precariously balanced between difficulties, and any change in the status quo makes them feel unsafe and angry. I think of the enslaved Hebrew people in Moses's time. When Moses went to Pharaoh for the first time to demand just a little bit of freedom—asking for a long weekend for a religious festival—and then when Pharaoh retaliated by increasing the people's workload, the people got mad at Moses. How dare you try to free us! They were not willing to risk the conflict. Even after they were freed, they looked back with nostalgia—the food was better in Egypt, they said. Better to be slaves, with good food, than to be free with nothing but this nasty desert food, manna, to eat. Healing and liberation can be very scary processes. And it can be advantageous for the powers that be—the pharaohs and the fossil fuel companies—to keep people desperate enough that they cannot summon the capacity to imagine or follow through with a big change.

Some people are not willing to start down the road of change, liberation, and healing. Perhaps they are "just scared" (as I judge from outside their hospital room) or perhaps their eyes are open to see all that is truly at stake, and they know they cannot pay that price. As I sat there in the hallway with Peter, crying over my anorexic patient, I realized there must be many things keeping her where she was. The tangles of trauma, an impossible load of societal expectations, perhaps a toxic family who prefer her to stay tiny and silent, and then if you throw in some sexism and fatphobia combined with her thoroughly wrecked metabolism and mixed with how little anyone knows about curing anorexia—shake and stir . . . and stand back. The disease that shared the hospital room with her that day was cunning, baffling, and deadly. It is as bad as cancer, as intractable as our fossil fuel addiction. It is appropriate for us to stand back in grief—and in anger, fear, and awe.

That day in the hospital hallway, grief was what I needed: to stand there, grieving how powerless I was to cure this anorexic patient. I needed Peter to sit with me and hold the space for me as I admitted how unmanageable the problem was, how deep, and how sad. And I needed support—Peter's company—to make me brave enough to visit her instead of keeping her on the end of the list. His support helped me step off the dock and take that small step into freefall even though it was not going to fix anything. His connection was critical.

As sea levels rise and the efforts of environmental activists roll powerlessly through the marble halls of government, we need to support one another. Whether that is in the face of the disease itself, looking the climate crisis in the eye, or in the integrity we decide to practice even though we know that cannot fix things, we need support. In the courage it takes to dive into the depths of vulnerability, we need someone to be there with us. In the daily decisions of where to go and who to see, in the discomfort of sitting in the patient's room, and in the freefalling grief of crying in the hallway afterward, we need to be connected to one another. We need our fellow swimmers on the dock with us, reaching out their hands, and counting down to "go." We can do very hard things if we do not do them alone.

Jumping into Grief

You have kept count of my tossings;
put my tears in your bottle.

—PSALM 56:8

Linnea was never just one of the crowd. An introvert, she clung to her best friend, Emma, in an extrovert-dominated youth group and got a little lost in the shuffle when Emma graduated a year ahead of her. She never had great drama to share at check-in time when many of the others would loudly lament about crushes and friendships gone awry. I would sometimes worry that her silence meant she felt unwelcome. Her tastes were different, too; she wanted to sing folk songs around the campfire, and although I loved the same old songs she did, we too often bowed to group pressure and stuck with the common-denominator pop songs for sing-alongs.

But when Linnea did speak, the whole group listened. She saved up her thoughts until she was ready, and everyone fell silent as her wisdom fell like a stone through the churning of other people's drama. She had been listening the whole time and knew exactly what to say. The others learned to respect her for it. When we dressed up one night for a youth group outing, she braided flowers into her long hair and pinned it up, circling her solemn face. The other girls seriously debated the question, "Which Greek goddess does Linnea most resemble?" in awe of not just her styling skills but her natural grace and poise.

Linnea went off to college in Santa Cruz, nestled between the ocean and great forests, where she found coursework perfectly matching her lifelong passion for the environment. At UCSC she biked from home to class to internship where she worked monitoring the health of small species in the forests. By the end of her education, she was organizing programs and events for her fellow future conservationists.

When college students come home on a break or over the summer, I usually meet up with them for coffee. But Linnea and I fell more quickly into the habit of taking a walk in the park nearby. She would bring her dog and we would hike between the redwoods just a few blocks from her house. She was much more at home there among the trees than in the noisy chatter of a café. Being a native New Yorker, I usually set a relatively fast walking pace and slow down for others, but Linnea is a cross-country runner and a head taller than me, so it was she who kindly curbed her athleticism to match my speed.

As we walked, I asked curious questions to try to get a glimpse of her life. She told me about her internship work, about supervising younger students who did not always take their work seriously, about the newts whose populations they were tracking, about the birds making a nest near her window at home. She told me about the good possibility her work would lead to a job placement and her hope that it would be fieldwork and not office work. I told her about my ideas for this book, and she was full of her own curious questions as she took them in.

I had many conversations to bring this book to fullness. Most were with extroverts whose ideas burst out in rapid speech like popcorn popping. True to her style, though, Linnea listened to my ideas first, took her thoughts home, pondered them in her heart, and then wrote me messages that spoke straight to the core. I quote her here in full:

> I'm planning to devote my career to saving species, but sometimes it feels . . . not even like I'm fighting an uphill battle, but like we've already lost the battle and I'm trying to salvage the scraps of what's left over. It's really painful for me to think about. When I had my fieldwork fellowship, I did informational interviews with employees there. I asked them how they deal with climate grief when their careers are so focused on the destruction of our environment, hoping they could offer me some advice. The advice that felt most emotionally resonant came from a woman who told me that working on climate change is distressing and depressing and there's not really a way around it. She told me that she and many other biologists who work on climate change issues deal

with a lot of pain, and it's just a choice I have to make on whether I'm willing to take that on. It was a sad answer to hear, but I felt relief to find someone to tell me that hard truth and who seemed to have dealt with a similar grief to mine.

To me, nature feels like the core of my identity. My life centers around nature: my career path is in conservation; my hobbies are hiking, backpacking, birding, and plant identification; my art is mostly paintings of nature. For me, it's hard to separate who I am from my love for nature. Climate grief is intertwined with my own sense of self, which can be very painful.

Growing up, I used to believe in a more traditional sense of God but lost that in my teenage years. These days I view nature itself as the divine. So for me, it feels almost like God is dying.

A chill of recognition ran down my spine when I read Linnea's message. She put so clearly what I muddled around to express. But of course she did. Where I was wading around knee-deep in ecological issues, she was already plunging into the deepest of waters. As I read and reread her wise words, the next-to-last lines of the musical *Godspell* echoed in my head: "O God, you're dying." I felt this mournful cry reverberate and resonate throughout my body. Like the panic and shock and grief when my mother was diagnosed with a rare and aggressive cancer. Except it is not just my mother, but all of our mothers—it is Mother Earth, who is one of the clearest windows I know to look through to the divine mystery behind it all.

When the Greek goddess Artemis was young, it is said that she hung on her father Zeus's knee asking for special assignment in her divine realm: "Give me all the mountains, Daddy; and for a city, assign me any city whatsoever: for seldom is it that Artemis goes down to the town. On the mountains will I dwell."[1] She was the protector of wild spaces. I am still trying to answer that riddle—Which Greek goddess does Linnea best resemble?—and I think Artemis is it. But Linnea is, alas, as human as the rest of us, despite her passion and wisdom. No deity will hand her the unlimited power to protect her beloved mountains. And we are all caught, with her, in a perpetual Good Friday, watching God die over and over again.

When I find myself wavering on the edge, not wanting to even read an article about the latest ecological devastation, I remember that Linnea is out there swimming in it, and it makes me braver. When I hold back from getting into a contentious argument about divesting from fossil fuels, I remind myself that the climate is being crucified on these issues, and so I jump in anyway. Minimizing the weight of these issues is not helpful; they are as important, as Linnea said, as the loss of self and the death of God. We each must pace ourselves, choosing a speed that will not exhaust us too quickly. And we need to remember who is swimming with us, that others' hearts are breaking too, and that others are mustering up all the courage and strength they have. Nobody needs to do this work alone.

---

1   Callimachus, *To Artemis*, lines 8–9. My translation of the Greek text found in *Callimachus, Hymns and Epigrams; Lycophron; Aratus* (New York: G. P. Putnam's Sons, 1921).

Part Two

LEARNING TO FLOAT

This is my prayer, that your love may overflow more and more.

—PHILIPPIANS 1:9

My mother says I learned to swim in a pond near Boston where we were visiting family. She says I jumped up and down in the water until at some point I realized I could stay up, without touching the bottom, by kicking and paddling a little. I do not remember this at all, though at six years old I was big enough to remember many things. What I do remember, however, is the feeling of people trying to teach me to swim by floating first. I could not float. I remember how scary it was as they coached me to put my head back and puff up my skinny belly with air and relax. Buoyancy did not come easily to me. To this day I am more comfortable treading water than floating.

Floating is a necessary skill, though, if you are headed out for a long swim. And the work of helping and healing our climate will be a long swim indeed—a long and a hard one.

We will need to take breaks, to roll over and face the sky and entrust our tired bodies to the grace of the water, for a time at least.

Spiritually speaking, learning to float is learning to believe we are beloved and to trust that we belong. When we feel well loved, affirmed, and accepted by others and by God, we develop a kind of spiritual buoyancy that will be there for us in the long haul ahead. We will be able to take breaks and rest, letting go of our striving for a time without falling into despair. Our attitude will become less frantic, our strokes more relaxed, as we realize we can pull and glide rather than thrashing endlessly around.

Floating needs to be learned from the inside out. It is not something you can learn theoretically. You can look at happily floating people all day long and still have no idea how to make it happen to your own body. The same with love. It is not enough to know what love looks like; you need to feel it within. Still, an encounter with someone who feels well loved, whose spiritual buoyancy is plain for all to see, can be inspiring.

I expected several things of the Reverend Dan Paul, pastor of the Christian Church (Disciples of Christ) in Pacific Grove and director of the Blue Theology mission trip program. I expected him to be calm and flexible. His emails, ahead of the trip, had frequently signed off with "let's remember to be fluid" and a water emoji. I expected to enjoy him. I knew his warm and peaceful voice from a few phone calls prior to our trip, and I suspected that he might be an excellent musician (indeed he was). But still, I was unprepared for the overflowing welcome Dan gave us that Sunday morning as we arrived, about a half hour before church, calling out in a booming voice as sleepy youth piled out of the cars, "Welcome! Welcome! Anyone want a latte?"

In the event that any of my readers have never had a cup of church coffee, or in case it has been a couple of years, I will remind you that it is famously bad: bought in bulk, stored haphazardly, used only once a week, and brewed by rotating amateurs. Never before, and never since, have I seen a full-on espresso bar in a church fellowship hall.

We muddled out of our cars and blinked sleepily at Rev. Dan, not sure what kind of a joke this was.

"I'm serious, folks! What can I get ya?"

We looked at one another.

"For real?" Mimi muttered to me. "An actual latte?"

"Am I dreaming?" Melvie cocked her head and asked the sky.

"I'll take one," offered Jim, our chaperone and lay pastor and part-time comedian. We followed curiously, thinking that if it was a joke, then at least Jim would have an excellent comeback. But no, it was for real. With a flourish, Dan asked Jim to pick a mug from the collection of church mugs (you know, half a hundred mugs netted from an assortment of denominational events, vacation spots, and local businesses), busied himself at the knobs of the machine, and poured Jim an actual latte.

"Come on, anyone else? What do you want?" Dan was eager to make us feel at home, and although his welcome was far more generous than how any of us expected to be treated at home, we could not turn him down. He was clearly delighted to be showing off his coffee skills. I giggled like the teenagers as I gratefully took my latte.

"It wasn't a fancy coffee church before I got here," Dan said. "But when they got to know me in the interview, they found out how much I love a good cappuccino. And when I arrived, they had bought this machine."

Pastor Dan's love language is good coffee. His congregation loved him and showed that love tangibly in the extravagant purchase of the espresso machine. And Dan's cup, running over, abundantly filled ours to the brim. What a waterfall of love.

Chapter 5

Like Nature's Hugging You

I remember the first time I went on retreat, the
sheer awe I felt from being there at Camp Caz. That
particular place just makes me so happy and makes
me feel really safe. Just going to the chapel, I think
I almost cried when I went there because it was so
beautiful. You're looking out, it's a little cliff-type
thing, but then you are surrounded by trees, and
it's like nature's hugging you.

—OLIVIA, sixteen

Our first spiritual need is the need for love and belonging.
In our hearts, we yearn to know the warm embrace of someone (or some One) who cares deeply about us, who sees us
and loves us just as we are, and to whom we belong. When this
need is well met, we feel secure in love, like swimmers who
float free, eyes closed, knowing the water holds them up. We
feel that we belong in the world.

Our spiritual needs are longings as deep as the ocean, so it may seem glib to speak of "meeting" such a spiritual need. It is not a problem that you can cure; it is a struggle we learn to live with. We will always tend to sink in the deep waters of chaos around us and will need to return again and again to the work of floating. That said, it is helpful to describe the ways in which our spiritual needs can be met while understanding that neediness does not vanish when they are met. Perhaps the way we "meet" our spiritual needs is more like "meeting" a person on the road than like "meeting" a requirement.

The first spiritual need gets met when people care about us; especially when they pay attention to us, compliment us, or somehow show that they see us in particular and love us.

Everyone has different love languages, of course, and what is bliss to some people may not register a blip on another's radar. Some like to hear love in words; some like to see it in action. Others treasure gifts, rites of passage, or shared experiences. We must recognize that love languages have generational as well as cultural variations, like spoken languages that may sound a little different depending on your region. A teenager spoke up during a youth group session on the topic, saying "memes are my love language." They did graciously explain the basic definition of "meme" to the two baby boomer adult advisors who were there with us that day, but I emailed the boomers some remedial memes the next day to help them catch up. That was love, though: recently retired people struggling to catch up with internet phenomena for the sake of the youth. Like parents learning a few words in their foster child's native language, they may never be fluent, but the effort is appreciated. No matter what love languages we are fluent in, we do our best to shower one another with different ways of communicating the truth that God loves you and so do we. You belong to God and you belong to us.

When I began pastoring at Montclair I inherited a sacred cow—an untouchable, unchangeable tradition: writing affirmations. At the end of every youth retreat, at the closing celebration, they would pass their program journals around for what seemed like forever, each writing a brief positive message to as many of their fellow retreaters as possible. At first I did not understand what powerful magic this was. The teenagers loved it so much and begged for more time to write affirmations, but it seemed to me that they were just nostalgically trying to prolong the retreat and avoid getting in the vans to go down the mountain. I told them they could pass the journals around in the vans if they needed more time. But it was not long after the retreat that I found myself reading and rereading my own booklet of affirmations. Sure, some of them were as eloquent as "thanks 4 the retreat u r cool," but enough of them touched deep enough to let me know that the youth had really seen me, loved me, and appreciated me. My favorite included a cartoon caricature of Rev. Talitha, so I guess I got clear that cartoons are my love language. Seven years later and I have never thrown out a single one of those program journals; the file folder is getting thick. Recently, at brunch with several of the alumni, we were reminiscing on retreats past, and one of them was marked by "Oh, that retreat was the one when we lost Zoe's journal somewhere on the van ride and never got it back." Silence fell. Oh, *that* retreat. The disaster was remembered with solemnity so many years later. Heads slowly shaking. A tragedy indeed.

This spiritual need for love and belonging can also be met when a group welcomes you in. We might think of formal rites like membership and baptism, when you get brave enough to stand in front of the whole community and affirm your common faith and hear the community promise to accept and love you and nurture your spirit. There the community holds you up for a time in prayer, and when the day has passed, you still feel held, raised up, floating in their love. But sometimes this feeling arrives in more personal and haphazard ways. One young woman speaks of the moment she knew she belonged at our church: someone asked for something in the church kitchen, and she knew where to find it (birthday candles, I believe, for a celebration). I remember when I knew I belonged in a new dance group: someone told me I had been missed at a practice. I blinked, surprised. Yes, of course I had skipped practice. . . . I had thought everyone knew I was down with a sprained ankle and would be useless for dancing for a couple of weeks. What use was it to show up to practice and just sit on the sidelines? But it was not my dancing they missed; it was me. I was surprised to know I belonged to them already.

When this spiritual need is met, we are secure. We know that, at least to someone, we are special. We do not think too little of ourselves; we are more or less right sized. Even in a really big universe, we know that we have our place and that we belong. With the psalmist, we can look at "the sun and the moon that you have established" and know that, in God's eyes, we too are "crowned with glory and honor" (Ps 8:3,5). If you were lucky enough to have had a good church retreat or summer camp experience as a child, you probably remember what it was like to stare up at the night sky and feel like one glorious piece of an incomprehensibly glorious whole. Like Olivia felt on retreat, you have a sense that nature reaches out and embraces you, lifts you up. When we are deeply loved we can have a feeling of awe that is not separate from ourselves; we too are special creations worthy of awe.

When this spiritual need is met, we are confident. Like a child who has been passed from arms to loving arms around the circle of community, we know that we matter to someone. If we speak up, we expect to be heard. If we suffer, we know that others will want to respond; if we rejoice, we expect others to be attuned to our joy.

Our spiritual need for love and belonging can (of course) be met in healthy families and friendships as well as in faith communities; but our need can also be exacerbated there if we meet with people who reject us, hurt us, or are indifferent to us. A little teasing at school—for anything from acne to bigger issues like disability, poverty, race, gender, or sexuality—knocks our self-worth down a few levels. Religious leaders who abuse their power to intimidate can do serious harm as well. This first spiritual need can be met rather simply if we are surrounded by people who love and appreciate us, but sadly we must all recognize how rare that can be.

If this need is not met, we sink. When it is more profoundly unmet—if we feel deeply unloved and unbelonging—we end up with such low self-esteem that we are unable to honor, appreciate, or even recognize the longings of our own spirit. We are always trying to rise back up to the surface of the water, kicking off the bottom. We may seem tense, insecure, or codependent, focused on others, and eager to please. If a stranger visits your church with this spiritual need deeply unmet, they are not likely to speak about it directly . . . because they probably know nothing about it. They may know that they feel lonely and disconnected, but they are likely to think it is somehow their fault. They tread water more and more vigorously to try to stay afloat. If they try to win a place at the church, they might end up taking on far more service commitments than they need to and posturing to prove that they are worthy to earn their membership. If we try to minister to them in the depth of this need, we will need to constantly assure them that we like them, value them, and genuinely enjoy them—not for what they can do, but for who they are. If we are successful, and their heart is open, we may eventually see them relax into a sense of belonging and let God's love embrace them.

I have a thousand stories about this need myself. I know what it feels like to be sunk deep in this unmet need. I have walked around the world with a huge bag of unbelonging on my back, so big it knocks people over if I try to turn around in a crowded café. I never see it, of course, but I know it is there because of the way I am constantly asking other people to reassure me I belong. I spent six months of my hospital chaplain residency apologizing for being new. That was six of twelve months, and even after I stopped apologizing I still did not really feel I had earned the right to be in the same room as the medical staff I worked alongside, much less to sit at the table and speak up about my insights.

There are so many reasons this spiritual need might be unmet. God knows we hurt one another deeply, with everything from sarcastic jokes to spiritual abuse. We hurt one another indirectly too; poverty and violence surround us and drag us down even when they do not touch our lives personally. And we hurt one another in this same indirect way with the massive global wound of the climate crisis. The climate crisis has left a generation (and more) feeling profoundly unloved.

Growing up during times of ecological catastrophe can make it hard for young people to have a robust sense of dignity. It is hard to float in waters where you are constantly being bumped by random flood debris, the wreckage of others' tragedies reduced to flotsam, now just collateral damage from one ecological crisis or another. It is hard to feel like you are beloved when you live in a trash heap. This is true of our neighborhoods, and it is true of our world. If we live in neighborhoods full of boarded-up windows, absentee landlords, and uncollected trash, we have a hard time believing we deserve better. If we live in a world marked by absentee politicians, overflowing landfills, and abandoned civic institutions, we will get used to our dreams meeting disappointment. Watching another forest fire and another species extinction and another neighborhood lost to flooding, we sink down into cynicism. If we come of age in a world on fire, it is hard to believe we are beloved children of God.

The young people of today are fighting not just the normal battles of insecurity, instability, and social challenges but also a global insecurity that affects them as subtly and surely as the air we breathe. They watch while the people in power do not even try to avert the climate emergency, and they interpret this as a message from the older generations saying their lives are not worth fighting for. I asked fifteen-year-old Elvin why he skipped school to go to the climate strike, expecting (from my millennial point of view) an answer like "protecting the environment is the right thing to do," but his Generation Z answer was much more to the point: "I don't want to die."

In middle school I had classes on self-esteem. Some educator somewhere had decided that this was a thing that could be taught to preteens, and so we spent a couple of classes with our health teacher (yes, the same one who had earlier shown us how to awkwardly put a condom on a banana) talking about the importance of looking in the mirror, looking past the skin and its flaws, and liking—even loving—what you see. I and my few friends seemed to come away from that with a sense that we were doing yet another thing wrong: that not only were we ugly, useless, untalented—the typical middle school insecurities—but we were also failing at the important task of loving ourselves.

Just like self-esteem, this sense of being beloved and belonging is not easy to teach or learn. The best thing you can do is to find a person who genuinely likes you for who you are and not what you do to earn their favor. It could be a teacher, a family member, a peer, or a partner (whether the relationship lasts long or not).

My husband was salvation to me here. I remember the first time he came to hear me preach. I was in seminary, we had been dating only a while, and he took a morning off work to hear me preach at a weekday chapel service. I had fussed endlessly over my sermon and I wanted to wow. Well, he admired me all right, but not for any of my written words, nor their polished delivery, nor my well-coordinated choices of musical settings. No: he loved my black robe and the curl in my hair. He loved my nervous smile and the way I tripped and recovered on the way up to the pulpit. Eventually, I was able to understand, with my mind blowing gaskets at every bump on the way, that he loved me for who I was, no matter what I did. I was beloved. I belonged.

I have seen it in others too, and sometimes even more dramatically. I love watching the sudden spiritual integration when one is known and loved. It rushes in from "Oh, this person loves me" to *"Everything in the universe loves me! And I love it too!"* I have seen an agnostic older teenager, who basically attended church to sing and do service projects with his friends, turn into a mystical young man who consulted God about everything. No coincidence that this transformation happened at the same time as a new romantic relationship unfolded. Being loved is such a strengthening experience. We stand taller, feel prouder, have more to give—and more to lose. Everything becomes more precious and beautiful.

But what if we have not fallen in love? What if we have never found the right person, with whom it was safe to open up? What if the people around us just do not speak love in a way we can hear and understand? How will this spiritual need be met if we cannot find that unicorn: a soulmate who loves us for who we are?

The good news is that this person could always be God. We need a little bit of spiritual imagination, but all we have to do is hear the message and receive it: you are God's child, God's delight, fearfully and wonderfully made, with all your quirks and insecurities, your impatience, your zits, and your bony elbows. And God is especially fond of you. A loving and embracing church community can help you really believe that: you are God's special child, beloved and blessed. You belong here.

Can we hear that assurance on a communal level—on the level of the human species? Can we also hear the message and receive it for ourselves: we are God's children, God's delight, fearfully and wonderfully made, with all our sins and wrongdoings, our addiction to fossil fuels, our wars, our prejudice? And God is especially fond of us. Oh, we have committed wrongs to repent of, no doubt, as surely as the teenager in the mirror needs to repent of picking at his zits and calling himself ugly. But down at the core, can we hear the message of ultimate belovedness? God's love surely had the first word, and we people of faith do hope that it will also be the last. Can we hold on to this good news in the face of our despair?

In non-Covid times, I volunteer at the Children's Hospital, three miles downhill from the church. I have an easy bike ride down, breezing past parks. The ride back home is much harder—uphill all the way—a good way to sweat out my angst if the hospital visits have broken my heart a little bit. I bring Godly Play stories with me, illustrations in paper and felt, which I spread out on the blankets or bedside tables of the young patients. Mostly I like to tell the parables, those beautiful, open-ended stories, which in Godly Play tradition are always kept in golden boxes (because something precious is inside). But one Saturday I made an unexpected swerve and told the Creation story instead. Some instinct had told me to change plans. I got on my bike to head to the hospital and thought I would pick up a few extra parable boxes at the church office on my way. When I got to the church office, I saw the Creation story. Before my brain knew what I was doing, my hands were busy making color photocopies and slicing them up at the paper cutter. Each Creation story is told using seven colored cards in a black linen envelope, which we lay out one by one as we tell the story and then give away for the kids to keep. As I sliced the cards, the paper cutter whooshing, I rehearsed and repeated the story in my head. "On the first day, God gave us the gift of light." *Slice.* "The gift of water . . . not just the water in the tap, or in the Bay, or even in the ocean, but the water from which all water comes." *Whoosh.* "The gift of creatures that walk on two legs, or four, or six or eight or a hundred." *Fold and tap.* "And God said it was very good."

It felt so good to stop and remember how beautiful the story could be as I laid it out on a child's bed. How nice it felt to say over and over again, "God said it was good."

Pablo on the oncology unit was drawn most to day three and its trees. He had a story to tell me about the redwood tree in front of his house and how it kept pushing up new seedlings all around. We sat in the window seat and he pointed out trees in the neighborhood—trees much smaller than *his* tree.

Charity, next door, wanted to take the pages out of the envelope herself. She pulled each one out with relish. "Oh, look! You're going to like this one," she said to me as she handed me day five, with its birds and fish.

Sara lay still in the ICU, mysteriously paralyzed, and told me the most important day was day six: when the animals and people came. Her favorite animals? Golden retrievers.

Amir could not talk well, though he nodded; his new medication made him loopy. But after the story, when he was asleep, his mother put her hand on day seven—the day of rest—and told me how much she longed to have the whole family home together on Sunday again.

Ximena, my oldest patient that day at fourteen years old, loved day four with the moon and stars . . . just like the night sky at summer camp, she said. I brought out some colored pencils, and we drew nature scenes and chatted about camp memories until her grandma arrived to visit.

Maybe that was what I needed that day, to tell five children the story of Creation so that by the time I finished I would have pronounced "God said it was good" thirty-five times in all. And five sweet children in various degrees of serious illness agreed with God and me. How could the world be anything *but* good, when it contains such wonders as redwoods and fish? Days of rest, and golden retrievers, and summer camps? There in the hospital, rising high over the streets and highways and train tracks of Oakland, we could look out and see the sky, all blue with puffy clouds and flocks of birds and a faraway mountain. The beauty of the day embraced us, lifted us to float away in the sky with the precious sparrows. We were just as beloved as all those wonderful creatures. We belonged in this beautiful world. Who could ask for anything more?

Chapter 6

A New Name

To everyone who conquers I will give some of the
hidden manna, and I will give a white stone, and
on the white stone is written a new name that
no one knows except the one who receives it.

—REVELATION 2:17B

I left church in a foul mood. I did not stay for fellowship. I did
not go around to parishioners to offer any appointments for
visits. I am not sure I even made eye contact with anyone on
the way out of the Lostine Presbyterian Church (est. 1888) and
its white clapboard walls.

As their pastoral intern, I usually had a lot of fun on Sunday
mornings. I had people to see (and hug) and ideas to discuss.
The coffee at fellowship hour was nothing to write home about,
but the hosts always put out real cream and homemade cookies.
I usually left high and happy. If anyone noticed my scowl, they
would have noted it: not typical.

But church had not been typical that morning. A group had been meeting at the church for a retreat, and their leader had been our guest preacher that morning. He had ruffled my spiritual feathers quite the wrong way and done nothing to soothe them back down again by the end of his sermon. Sitting through the closing prayers and hymns in this mood had just intensified my angst.

Stormily I walked back to the manse, a whole hundred feet across the lawn from the church, and slammed the screen door. After a committed but unsuccessful attempt to eat my feelings, I gave up, closed the fridge, and called a friend to complain.

My complaint was homiletical. I had suffered through preaching malpractice. The preacher had talked about the passage from Revelation that says, "I will give you a new name." To the one that is victorious, God will give a white stone with a new name written on it. The people who had been on the retreat had all received their new names, carefully chosen by the leaders. They had actually gone so far as to make them new nametags. And the little country church buzzed with the spiritual energy of people who had been told they could hear God call them "Forgiven," and "Empowered," and "Precious." They wore their nametags proudly. They were not just floating on this love; they were practically high.

But none of these were *my* new name, and the preacher did not give the rest of us more than a moment in passing to ask God for a new name. So I sat there listening to this sermon on how powerful it was to let God call you by a new name, and yet I still only had the name I had walked in with. I felt like a kid in a candy store watching others enjoy a treat I had not even had the chance to purchase. It was not fair, or right, or *nice*, or good preaching.

My friend on the phone was pragmatic, though, and after a certain amount of listening to me complain she just interrupted. "So, Talitha, if God gave you a new name, what would it be?" I had to think for only a moment; it was on the tip of my tongue. It had been on the tip of my tongue the whole time. I just opened my mouth and said it: "God's beloved." She got goose bumps, my friend said, because it was on the tip of her tongue too. She knew it was my name.

From that time onward, I knew that "God's beloved" was my secret name. I knew without a doubt that it was what God called me, and how the divine eyes saw me. My soul answered to this name.

That does not mean it was easy to internalize the message of the name. "God's beloved" was a good name for me because it did not come easy. I wrote it on my bathroom mirror and practiced calling myself by it; I contemplated it and tried to truly learn it. I would catch myself, out in the world, acting as if I were not God's beloved, and I would stop and call to my soul like a parent calling a wayward toddler.

But other than my friend, who remembered the shared and holy moment on the phone, I did not tell it to anybody else. It was several years later when I first outed myself as I told the story to a group of colleagues. They were my fellow chaplains at the University of California (San Francisco) Medical Center, and we were getting to know one another by telling spiritually significant life stories. I told them about that day at that little country church, with the guest preacher and the phone call and the new name. Everybody nodded appreciatively.

And one asked, "So that must be what Talitha means, then?"

She was quite confident the answer was yes.

"Oh, no." I hastened to straighten things out. "Talitha is a biblical name, and I have had it all my life. I mean that 'God's beloved' is my spiritual secret name."

"Oh," she said, disappointed.

And I blinked and thought again. Why was it a secret?

Sitting across from me was a transgender man who had changed all three of his names at a spiritually important time in his life. Could I not do the same? I supposed I could. Still, I filed it under "nice ideas" and left it there for a long time. . . . Until one day in premarital counseling, I saw my fiancé's eyes get moist when he confessed what a big deal it would be if I took his last name. I hemmed and hawed, and we bargained over it for a while. Eventually, the memory of my transgender colleague's spiritual freedom to take *three* new names cut through and set me free. I took two. I kept my first name, changed my last to my husband's, Aho, and took on a new middle name: Amadea. Amadea was the closest Latin translation I could find for the name that came through, clear as a bell, on that phone line that day: God's beloved.

So now it is on *all* my nametags. No longer just a private name on the bathroom mirror, it is now public. People ask me what it means and I answer: I am God's beloved. I still have to practice remembering it, of course. Believing I am beloved does not come naturally to me; I have always been prone to the kind of perfectionism that makes me think I need to *earn* some higher status before I can think of myself as beloved. But this name was an unconditional gift. I am ever thankful that the name came through to me on the phone line not on a day when I had made a great achievement or breakthrough or even performed an act of selfless service. It came to me just where I was: in the worst of moods, on a door-slamming kind of cranky day. It was not earned or deserved; it just *was*.

Now the climate crisis takes the name game to a new level. If I have haltingly practiced and gotten better at saying, "I am God's beloved," I have even less regularly practiced saying, "We are God's beloved," but that is what we need to muster up for now.

I struggle to believe that we human beings are beloved of God. So many unlovable things are on full display: our greed, our apathy, our selfishness. We can only look at the climate crisis for so long before we realize that the problems are not scientific at the core or even technological. The problems are moral: people simply do not want to sacrifice now to have a better life in the future. Those with the power to divert this crisis just do not care enough about others to make a difference. We have all the science we need to clean up and cool the earth, and new technologies are being invented every day, yet we do not have the political will to activate these alternatives. People of goodwill are barely able to "green up" their own lifestyles, focusing on the small things that can be controlled—consumer asceticism or dietary improvements—while the unyielding economy continues to demand more on a large scale.

I struggle to see humanity as beloved of God when we as a species have done so much wrong, so publicly. If we could excuse ourselves, looking at the climate crisis as if it were the result of pure ignorance and naïvely saying, "If only we had known," we might be able to hold on to an unshaken sense of God's love. But our human failings, particularly the failings of the so-called developed world, are on full display. It was not ignorance of the harms of fossil fuels but plain greed for profit that plunged us into an ever-escalating dependence on the dirtiest of fuels. Gas companies researched the possible harms of carbon emissions, looked at the results, and decided to bury them deep. The rest of us read the news, shook our heads in wonder and dismay, and kept on buying air conditioners and new cars. People knew—and wrecked the world anyway. At times like these it is convenient to have a faith that speaks of sin, and perhaps even of "total depravity," the doctrine that says humans are fallen, failed, thoroughly beyond their own efforts to make things better. If we believe this, we can skip straight to a cynical acceptance, saving precious time that otherwise would have been spent wondering whether people would "do the right thing," only to be disappointed when they did not.

We need to learn to look at humanity in the mirror on the worst days—the door-slamming cranky days—and know we are beloved, not because we have done anything to deserve it, but because God's love for us is even bigger than our failings.

We need to spend time resting in the enormity of God's gracious love. Perhaps we will even be able to believe that God's steadfast love could be bigger than the climate emergency, wider than a fully trashed earth, deeper than the worst we can do.

Chapter 7

Better Not to Have Been Born

We were given such an intricate wonderful thing to shepherd, and we are killing it. I mean, killing it in a bad way, not like slaying.

—LUCIE, twenty-one

Tracy came to spill her guts. I had spoken recently in church about "the pain of loving the world," and that was what she was struggling with. We met at lunchtime on the walking trail near church, where we found a bench and opened our lunches. Tracy took one bite of her sandwich and then launched into a torrent of story. Her spiritual pain was so much deeper than her hunger that she spoke for twenty minutes straight, gulping air between sentences, before she took a second bite of the sandwich. The pain of loving the world was not just the question of the day; it was her life story. It had started with her very serious campaign, in second grade, to save the whales. And it continued now when she found herself fearing for her young daughters' future. She knew the odds of our keeping global temperatures down. She knew them and wept over them. The terror of our recent fire season had wrecked her; the animals that had not been evacuated from the Paradise fire broke her heart.

As she talked it became clear to me that she was in emotional pain all the time and could never do enough to cure or even soothe it. She tried working as an activist but was only more frustrated; she tried withdrawing but was plagued with guilt. The suffering around her, to which she was so keenly attuned, was making her depressed on behalf of all humanity.

A science-fiction series I enjoy has a class of telepaths particularly gifted in empathy; when someone gets so powerful that they can attune to anyone around them, they are called empaths. That certainly was Tracy's superpower. Anyone else's suffering could be hers, whether it was her daughter trying to get through elementary school or the latest news of turtles found dying with plastic in their stomachs. The rest of us could use a few lessons in empathy from her; but in such a broken world, it is hard for anyone to wear this superhero cape. She plainly needed relief.

Once she had poured out her heart into my pastoral hands, she sighed and asked me, "So how do *you* handle the pain of loving the world?" and bit into her sandwich. It was my turn to talk.

I sat there, humbled by her trust. I thanked her for her story and affirmed the things she was doing well. I really did not know what to say, but her mouth was full and mine was not, so I just kept talking. And after casting about for a bit, I said something she hooked on to: "The Bible says all this suffering—'the groaning of creation'—is like labor pains. It feels intolerable, but it's for a purpose. Somehow, even if we can't see it, we're working all together to bring some new life into existence; it's like one big global push. And on the other side, there will be something amazing . . . like we'll level up somehow and be liberated to be more of who God created us to be. But we have to push through the labor right now."

"That's always been a hard metaphor for me," she said with her mouth full. "Did a man write that?"

"Ha! Yes, we're pretty sure Paul was male."

"It seems romanticized. I'll tell you, when I gave birth to my kids, I really wanted to do it all natural. And for the most part, I did. But both times, the labor wasn't what I was hoping for. I mean, I got healthy babies out of it without having to take pain meds myself, so I got what I wanted . . . but secretly I hoped it would be a transcendent experience. I hoped it would teach me that ultimately pain was okay in the grand scheme of things. Like all the pain I'd held in my heart before that, the vigils for the prisoners, the campaigns to save the whales, all of that was just an attempt to get at the mystery of suffering, but I'd never truly—truly!—suffered myself. So I wanted to go down deep into the pain of labor and come back up knowing that all the suffering is ultimately worth it, that it all unfolds according to some beautiful divine plan. And I didn't experience it that way. It was just . . . well, it was excruciating. I got through it, but it wasn't okay at all."

"But the pain *was* worth it, now, because you have your children." (I wish I had not contradicted her like that, but I did.)

"I don't know. I'm not a sentimentalist. What's their future going to be like, you know?"

I didn't know. Sara and Patricia seemed like happy children to me.

"They love church, so I guess you see them at their happiest, but there's so much more to it, and for Sara in particular, a lot of her life is really hard."

I fell silent a beat.

"But she is alive," I said gently.

"But she suffers so much," she said, with tears quickly jumping into her eyes.

It was true. Her daughter had several serious illnesses, which required painful treatments. I visited her when she was last hospitalized and saw her agony firsthand.

"Torture. Like crucifixion," Tracy had said to me back then, and I did not doubt her. When I preached that year on Good Friday and found it was my turn to speak about Mary at the foot of the cross for the subject of my sermon, it was Tracy who gave me a view into Mary's agony.

"I can't help wondering, would it have been better for her if she had not been born?"

She did not shy away from even this terrible question. She dug in further.

"And I wonder that same question about humanity. Wouldn't it have been better for the whole world if humanity hadn't arrived? Or if we were back at some point in history when we were just primitive people living in little communities on the land. Or maybe even before we stood upright and got these big heads and narrow hips that just *kill* us in childbirth. What a trade-off! I mean, wouldn't that have been better? Humans are ruining the world. We don't deserve to have the world entrusted to our care. And we're not going to survive this. Wouldn't it have been better not to even start?"

I was daunted. She was digging back into her sandwich: my turn to say something again. This time at least I was not going to contradict her.

"It's true. We've made some awful trades. Yes, we're getting smarter and creating more elaborate things, but we're wrecking the health of the world while we do it."

She nodded at me to go on. I floundered. I knew what worked for *me* but I was not sure it would work for her. I tried talking around it.

"I wonder whether a whole different kind of world would have been better, or a whole different kind of humanity. . . ."

She cocked her head—curious.

How could I say this? Sometimes you just have to come out with it.

"Do you read any science fiction?"

She shook her head but smiled. "I really just don't have time."

Well, that was a neutral reply, so I took it as a green light. You can never be sure when confessing that, as a Presbyterian pastor, a portion of your strength and hope comes from sci-fi. Some people laugh.

"Well, reading sci-fi, I can imagine all kinds of different planets out there with different kinds of life on them. I can question God's decision in creating a planet that's as chaotic as ours. I don't just mean human violence; I mean earthquakes, and volcanos, and fragile ecosystems and a volatile changing climate, and all."

She nodded but did not quite latch on yet.

"Here's what I mean. If we were on a different kind of world, we might be a different kind of people. One of my favorite authors wrote once about people on a huge, slow-changing planet. The ground was fertile and muddy, and the climate was gentle and stable. And humans had evolved there in a way that they made really long-range decisions. They thought in thousand-year terms. They weren't going to get caught in a petty national war as quickly and violently as we do. They wouldn't trash their planet like we've done."

Now she was nodding; she got the point. I felt relieved that I had not revealed the depths of my sci-fi geekery for nothing.

"And so I have to think, God *could* have created a world like that, and I mean, maybe God did—the universe is wide enough that it could be true somewhere else—but for sure God created *this* world, and so God must have wanted to create it . . . or thought it was worth the risk . . . even though the volcanoes and earthquakes are really awful. And even though the people who developed here are, well, the way we are. God must have chosen to make us this way, in all our chaos and violence, because somehow we are still wonderful, and good, and worth it."

Tracy was with me.

"And our planet is excruciating sometimes, if you live at the foot of a volcano or you live on a fault line—"

"Yeah," she pointed back toward the church and my house, which both sit directly on the Hayward Fault.

"But it also has the Himalayas and the Grand Canyon and the Amazon—"

"Too close." She frowned—the Amazon was currently on fire.

"Touché. Well, I mean, the earth has a lot of fragile wonders that we could ruin, that we are already ruining, like the endangered species, but in another sense, even our invasive species, the common stuff like dandelions, are also incredible because they're so tenacious and determined. Another sci-fi book I remember had aliens who didn't have flowers on their planet. And they just were insane over the flowers we had here."

She laughed.

"So if I imagine trying to hold God to account, to interrogate God for why we have to suffer so much, I imagine God answering by taking us back for a big-picture look at everything and showing us the best of ourselves. I imagine God saying, 'Look, you humans have your deep struggles. But you also have such great things . . . orchestras, and skyscrapers, and so many different kinds of festivals. You have so many heroes, in times of war as well as in peace, and such brave, loving, incredible people.' I feel like God can really be proud of us, even though God sees our faults too. And I'm not theologically sure whether God would say, 'This is the *only* place where I was so in love with you that I sent my Son to incarnate and live as you' because there could be other Christs on other planets—yikes, that's a whole other question—but just imagine God saying that. Imagine God saying, 'I am so in love with humanity that I wanted to become human myself.'"

Now the tears were jumping into *my* eyes. The incarnation gets me every time.

"And also, because God became human in Christ, God's not just out there watching us suffer. God feels the suffering with us."

"Yes." She was with me. Imagining God as a superempath like herself.

"But why—" she started. She choked up, took a breath, and started again. "If God suffers with us, then why wouldn't God stop it?"

I spread my hands in a gesture of uncertainty.

"Maybe it's too costly, somehow, too cruel to intervene. Like the loss of human freedom isn't worth it to God to fix it."

"Maybe," she said.

"Or the value of our finding our own way, even if we find our way through lots of suffering, is so precious in God's sight, enough to be worth more than all the suffering."

"Huh," she said, not convinced. The cost of suffering, for someone who feels it so keenly, must be a high price to pay indeed.

"Or, okay. Maybe . . ." I hesitated; this one is harder, theologically. "Maybe God can't. Maybe this was the risk God took in creating free beings like us, that now there are things that are not under God's total control. Like when you fall in love, and there's this other person there now who affects everything. And that's the price of being in relationship with another free human being. Or I imagine like when you have children. Your life isn't your own anymore."

"No, it's not."

"I hope God doesn't regret us, but it's possible. And there is the Noah's ark story, where God does regret everything and try to start over again."

"Honestly, if I were God, I might."

We folded our sandwich wrappers and walked on out; I took Tracy's brave questions home with me. They had put little roots down into my soul. I pondered: If I were God, would I wash the world out and try to start again, with a little less chaos and pain this time? If I were God, would I be proud of humankind or always sorrowing over our sins? I am no great empath myself; is God perhaps more like Tracy than like me, always suffering vicariously and wishing she could take the pain away? Is God dying every day, in agony with us? Or is God even less of an empath than either of us, a hands-off God, as our more deist friends believe—one who created the world and abandoned it to see what happens?

I have been interrogating God ever since. How do you really feel about your people, God? Are we, by any chance, your favorite mistake? Do you still "so love the world" now that we have so thoroughly wrecked it? Are we causing you unspeakable pain, or are you able to push through and bear it? Have you loved us even through our extinctions and genocides? Will you still love us tomorrow?

The answer has never come through as quick or as clear as "God's beloved" came through to me on the phone, but I believe the answer is the same: that we humans are God's beloved people, God's glory, God's delight. You can build a case for this thesis, Scripture by Scripture, story by story. Here you add Psalm 8: humans are "crowned with honor and glory" just a little lower than the angels . . . there you add a news story: evidence of great human creativity. Moments of heroism. Yes, you can include those clickbait feel-good stories or perhaps a beautiful and wise thing that a child says. Look for evidence, and you will find plenty. A lot about us is awe-striking and amazing.

Still, the best answer comes not from evidence at all. It does not come from earning, deserving, impressing, winning favor, or even from serving God. Those of us who are deeply needy—who struggle to keep a sense of belovedness and belonging—do best when we stop trying to earn or deserve anything and rest in the knowledge that we are loved just as we are. We do best when we stop frantically treading water and learn to just lean back and float in the grace that is around us. This applies in the big picture too. The more we worry about whether we humans are "good enough," the less likely we are to rest in God's unconditional love. But if something cuts through and gets us to stop counting, stop evaluating, and just rest in the goodness of undeserved love, we are much more quickly able to understand how loved we are. Human life, in spite of all its horrors, is still a precious thing. Just to be alive is a miracle, and to be alive at such a time as this is a humbling wonder.

The advice I offered Tracy that day, and indeed the tactic I usually use on myself, was to think of the great things that could counterbalance the awful things humans have done. We end up saying, "Ah yes, we do deserve the glory of this painful and beautiful life on earth." But that kind of evaluation, the good against the bad, will ultimately leave us as insecure as the person who looks in the mirror and counts good hair days against bad ones.

Christian tradition has long held that it is the grace of God and not our accumulation of good days or good deeds that counts. God's eyes have always been open to the depth of our evil as much as our good, and God has loved us still; loved us enough to send Jesus to make that grace knowable. We have done everything possible to *not* deserve what we have, and yet God sends blessings raining down on our heads, good and evil alike.

> *We know that the whole creation has been groaning in labor pains until now; and not only the creation, but we ourselves, who have the first fruits of the Spirit, groan inwardly while we wait for adoption, the redemption of our bodies.*
> —Romans 8:22–23

Creation groans even more loudly these days, and even though Tracy's critique stuck with me, I still use the verse from Romans in prayer, and I feel a sense of solidarity when I pray with "the whole creation." We pray groaningly for God to redeem us, not just spiritually, but physically, in our suffering bodies. When we endure heat waves, storms, and seasons of smoke, we pray to be released from these cycles of pain and futility. Our presbytery uses the same verse in our antiracism work as we pray for the redemption of Black and brown bodies, which carry too great a share of trauma and suffering. I set the verse to meditative music during my pregnancy and hoped to use it in my own labor, but my birth experience was too much like Tracy's—just plain painful. With my contractions coming every two or three minutes from the get-go, meditating on Scripture was out of the question.

The prayer that stuck with me in my own labor was far simpler. The night I went into labor, my four-year-old niece Junia said grace before dinner: "Dear God, it's so nice to have a new baby. Talitha's baby is being born, and we have radishes. Amen." She meant the radishes on the table, being an odd radish-loving child, but I interpreted her gratitude more existentially. A day or two later I shared her prayer with the new baby crying in my arms. "It's okay, baby," I crooned, "the world is hard and painful. There's a lot to cry about. But it's a good place too, and we have radishes."

Junia's prayer stays with me when the baby cries all night and I feel helpless, when I tremble in fear of wildfire, or when I watch a climate bill struck down in Congress. Often I cannot connect to the more complex vision articulated by Paul—the trust that our suffering is not in vain—but I can at least hold on to the joy of Junia, the faith of a little child. In her eyes, the miracle of childbirth is right up there with the miracle of radishes grown from grocery-store seed packets. Let the little children lead us, again, to find the joy in a plant, a snack, a simple slice of life; it is all miraculous, and none of it earned or deserved. A simple prayer like Junia's helps us float in God's love when the struggle of life is too much for us.

Chapter 8

Gaining Confidence

I remember feeling so at home, like with family, knowing I will really miss this community and thinking about how much it's brought to me and my good friends.

—JUSTINE, nineteen, reflecting on her final mission trip with the youth group

As a youth pastor, one of my favorite tasks is attending the young people's events. I love getting invitations to their musicals, soccer matches, graduations, and art shows. I get misty-eyed watching them sing in choruses and awe-struck as they swing from trapezes in the local circus. If I can find their family to sit with—or, even better, convince other youth group members to meet me there—we become a little cheering section and we shout embarrassingly loud. We cheer whether or not "our" player scores or "our" team wins. We embarrass them, of course, but we also watch them glow with pride: proud to have made the team (or the band), proud of their teammates, and proud to have fans in the stands.

All these events are belovedness boosters. They remind us that we belong to something big and proclaim that belonging in tangible ways: with uniforms, costumes, pomp and circumstance. Trips and retreats are also amazing ways to boost youth's sense of belovedness and belonging. Is it leaving home that brings us closer together? Is it the intensity of uninterrupted time together? The magic of doing kitchen chores? However new you might be, come on a retreat and by the end of the weekend, you know you belong and are loved—even before the van ride home when you open your journal and read the affirmations.

As we think about swimming the troubled waters of the climate emergency and gaining a sense of belovedness and belonging as floating, these events and retreats are every kid's friend: the floaties. Whether you learned confidence in the water while wearing blowup armbands, hanging onto a kickboard, or riding an inflatable unicorn, floaties are not just useful for learning to swim; they are also a lot of fun.

When Covid-19 struck, Generation Z lost a lot of their spiritual floaties. Wave after wave of cancelations broke on them, first slowly and then in a flood: no youth group retreat, no soccer games, no concerts, no in-person graduation. While those of us who provided online programming surely worked our hardest to make our offerings meaningful, I will be the first to say that an online mission trip (we called it a mission untrip) could not hold a candle to what we had planned in Mexico.

I admire the resilience of the young people I know; they have coped remarkably well. But I still wonder about the long-term impact of what they missed. Did having fewer extraordinary days teach them to value the ordinary? Or in the absence of these great days, is there some way they are able to lean back on the unconditional love of God, modeled by the love of people in their lives?

Though I know of nobody who says floaties are no fun, many swim teachers say floating aids are counterproductive. Like training wheels on a bike, they can give a child a false sense of security, and then they will be frustrated as they struggle to learn how to swim without the aids. Floating while holding onto a buoy is not quite the same thing as floating free with that deep relaxation it takes to trust the water. It would be better, they argue, to do early swimming lessons without the aids and only introduce them later for play.

So perhaps the folks of Generation Z, who missed out on so many spiritual floaties, will be okay anyway. Perhaps their loss will not affect their learning to swim, and perhaps they will even be more confident for having learned without external boosters. I still expect them to enjoy the events, the shows, the games, and the ceremonies when they return. And I will be there in the stands cheering for them.

I was a child at Camp Glenkirk, a wilderness camp run by the National Capital Presbytery. It had a lodge, a swimming pool, and all that, of course, but mostly we spent our time in the woods. We cooked over a fire. We slept in tents and treehouses with no more electricity than our flashlights. We hiked, canoed, swam, and played no-tech games with a few balls and bandanas. We told scary stories and sang old songs.

And we went barefoot. A rare treat, for me. The rest of the year I was a city kid—my feet never touched the ground. Not that I was above it all, carried around in taxis like Eloise. But the ground at home was too gross to touch, from the piss to the leaking garbage bags to the crack vials on the sidewalk. Going barefoot in New York City is a sign of probable insanity. So camp was amazing, for me. Footloose in the grass, I felt "grounded" through contact with the earth as we ran around for a week like little Adams and Eves.

The camp had little in the way of equipment or programming. The theory was to build Christian community in small-group ("village") living, and good counselors plus nature were all you needed. In arts and crafts, we picked up black walnut shells, sawed them open, and polished them down to make weird-looking necklaces. A big group project was to roast a ham overnight, buried in bonfire coals. An ambitious adventure was an all-day canoe trip with our lunches packed in dry bags. But though these projects and adventures were fun, the most amazing thing for me was the free time. Every morning featured "quiet time," sending us out solo and silent to contemplate God and Nature and Everything. Most afternoons included a good nap, flopping down somewhere on the grass or by the lake or even—carefully—in a canoe. And every evening, it seemed, we had time to stare at the stars. The world was so big! It was so awe inspiring! And it was so good. Floating in the magic of camp, we felt secure and loved.

I went back when I was eighteen as a camp counselor and learned a little bit about how to make this magic happen for a few hundred campers. First, safety (Safety! Safety!). In the years since I had been a camper, someone had invented a thing called liability insurance, and bare feet were a big no-no now (so much for the garden of Eden). Still, we could have fun if we stayed safe. We trained the children in our care, drilling them on water safety and teaching them the respectful use of fire. One week I gave an insect-education speech to a few young campers from the city, including the "watch out because ticks can suck your blood" piece. Not a half hour later we stopped everything, hushed, and pointed out a deer in the woods, at which point one very worried camper asked whether deer could also suck your blood. Reassure, reassure, reassure.

Then love, love, love. We made sure to rotate activities so everyone could play a game or do a craft that they were especially good at. We told them how amazing they were when they learned to cook over an open fire or steer a canoe. We watched them shine and made sure to beam love back at them. We made up corny village cheers or made matching tie-dye shirts to broadcast our sense of group belonging.

The rest was simple: a few songs and verses to give them deep thoughts about God; the majesty of the lake, the river, the sky. The fireflies and eagles and choruses of singing frogs all worked together to strike awe into their young hearts. We counselors invented a few dramatic tricks, like lighting a bon-fire with a single match, but mostly we stood back and let the kids enjoy nature, God, and one another.

The work was good for me. Even at age eighteen, worka-holism was already creeping its way into my life. I had taken twenty-one credits my first semester at college with a full load of extracurriculars; I had learned to run on fumes. So it was truly perfect that my work that summer was, literally, to play. It was constant and tiring work, still, and much less fun being the grown-up than the kid, but it was exactly what my soul needed. I unplugged from email. The closest I had to a cell phone was the camp walkie-talkie. I unplugged from stress and plugged in to nature. I was also much farther away from home than many other counselors, so I stayed put at camp most weekends as well, when other counselors went home and the camp was quiet. I walked and rested, read and thought. When nobody was there to enforce the new rules, I took off my shoes and walked barefoot, slowly, contempla-tively, grounding myself. I remembered the Sabbath day and kept it holy for once. I was badly overdue for Sabbath rest, and those weekends at camp forced me to do it.

I returned to college at the end of the summer full of songs, starry nights, and sweet memories; but more than that, I returned feeling secure and grounded in God's love. "This summer," I wrote in my journal, "the spark of God's love burst into a flame." The long days spent outdoors had uncurled me deep inside, warming and relaxing and opening me up to that eternal love.

> *Remember the sabbath day, and keep it holy.*
> *Six days you shall labor and do all your work.*
> *But the seventh day is a sabbath to the Lord*
> *your God; you shall not do any work—you, your*
> *son or your daughter, your male or female*
> *slave, your livestock, or the alien resident in your*
> *towns. For in six days the Lord made heaven and*
> *earth, the sea, and all that is in them, but rested*
> *the seventh day; therefore the Lord blessed the*
> *sabbath day and consecrated it.*
>
> —Exodus 20:8–11

Spending Sabbath-type time in nature, enjoying the goodness of creation, is an antidote to the busyness of ordinary life. The young people of today have been plunged quickly into the world of achievement and competition. We all know what it feels like: we work, and stress, and, when we are done, flip straight into consumption mode, watching movies, purchasing entertainment, and doom-scrolling through Twitter . . . or perhaps dreaming of the relaxing cruise we will take someday. We work hard, serving the world, and when we stop working, we want to be served, whether that is by uniformed waitstaff or by an ever-present app. We produce, and then we consume in turn. This system leaves us with a subtle wound in our confidence. We feel we are only worth as much as we contribute to the system.

The world might tell us that observing Sabbath is like taking a cruise—the leisure we purchase at the end of the week.

But Sabbath is not part of the produce-consume cycle at all. The word *sabbath* in Hebrew literally means "stop." This day of rest is nonproductive, nonconsumptive, subversive, and healing. It is a walk in the grass, a flop on a beach, an abundance of time. Sabbath is not a luxury that you can save up for. It cannot be captured or achieved. It is unconditional; a time to rest in the sheer fact of God's love for you.

In the Godly Play Creation story, day seven is a blank paper card with no symbols or instructions on it at all. Different people remember the gift of the seventh day in different ways, we say, whether that is going to church or synagogue or mosque or just settling somewhere in your own home. It could be any place special where you can give thanks for all the gifts that God has given us—a tree in the backyard or a mountaintop destination. Many children want to fill the card in with religious symbols—crosses and stars and such—but teachers are taught to resist that urge, leaving the seventh card blank and open, like the Sabbath itself should be. Can you imagine a whole day stretching before you?

Whether it happens on a Sabbath day or on your average Tuesday, spending nonproductive, nonconsumptive time in God's creation heals our souls in a way we profoundly need right now. The natural world is good for us, psychologically speaking. Our brains are hardwired to respond favorably to the sound of the ocean, the sight of tree branches, the smell of dirt. Our tightly wound achievement complexes slowly unravel in the presence of still water. Though we may worry about the health of the natural world, it still has the power to heal us.

Generation Z is missing out on this kind of nonproductive, nonconsumptive time spent in nature. Many of them lack time, as work, school, and extracurriculars pile on in a world of high competition for scant resources. The attention economy effectively wires them into their apps, constantly working to keep their eyeballs on the advertisements. Others grow up in areas without accessible wild spaces or even parks. Access to nature tracks with wealth, of course, and varies by race due to our nation's segregationist housing policies, and Generation Z, being the most racially diverse generation in our nation's history, is acutely aware of this division.

The ability to sit and contemplate a tree should not be a luxury. Falling down into the grass to come eye-to-eye with the wonder of a grasshopper should not be a right reserved for those who have purchased their own plot of grass. And everyone needs a day of rest—not to labor, not to side hustle, not even to perform for your app audience—just to simply be. Ultimately, we learn to relax and float in God's goodness and love by letting go of the need to do things well. Though our great achievements can give us confidence, our nonachievement days teach us how to truly rest and trust in the goodness that we do not need to earn.

Chapter 9

Beauty Makes a Difference

Going to such a beautiful place makes you appreciate nature. I have these memories, so it's something that would drive me to fight for nature.

—MELVIE, nineteen

In 2016 when our youth group was in Chicago for a mission trip, the organizers sent us out into the neighborhoods to do community gardening work. I am all about community gardening, but I got a little annoyed the first day when I saw where they were sending us. I stood there in the twenty-by-sixty-foot garden, listening to our orientation from a local Catholic deacon, and I had a lot to say. I bit my tongue and impatiently waited for my turn to speak up.

I know I am not the first person to go on a mission trip and want to explain to the people I am serving what they are doing wrong. And I know from my missiology classes that one ought not to do so . . . especially if one literally has an ancestry of colonizers. But in this case, what I had to say was important!

You see, they were not growing food in this garden. It was just flowers, bushes, nonfruiting trees, and shrubs. As I listened I internally prepared my speech about how much more useful it could be if it were a place of nourishment and not just beauty, how the berry bushes and fruit trees would be equally easy to grow, how meaningful it could be for hungry people to come and get a free snack. When they heard my wisdom, they would certainly change all their plans and transform the place. Luckily, I did not have a chance to interrupt before my half-listening ear caught this from the deacon:

> I came to this neighborhood when I was young. And the nuns had been working on this little garden for only a while; it wasn't what you see now. But even then, when it was just a few flowers, it made such a difference. Do you know what it's like to walk through your neighborhood and see nothing beautiful? Or to see ugliness? It gets to you, man. It makes your head hang down and makes you rush past in a hurry, not stopping to look at anything, just getting by. Do you know what that feels like?

Oh.

I did know.

The neighborhood I grew up in in New York City had a tiny pocket park on the corner. It featured thick ivy growing over everything, bits of trash thrown over the always-locked gates, thin weedy trees shooting desperately for the sky, and the biggest rats you have ever seen. They were bigger than subway rats! We called it Rat Park.

Now, this was not our neighborhood's only park—we could walk ten minutes to Central Park or five minutes to Riverside Park—but Rat Park was ours, our block's park, and the energy it gave off was infectious in the worst sense of the word. At best we could feel cool in bragging about how hardcore our urban environment was, but more typically we would feel depressed and grossed out by its awful conditions.

Okay, Mr. Deacon. I get it.

I swallowed my urban-agriculture speech unsaid. I dutifully clipped shrubs for the rest of the morning. I cheered for the teenager pushing the mower and encouraged those who were stuck in the weeds. As we worked, I slowly began to see the garden in a new light. It was beautiful indeed. It had places to sit, shade and sun, and the layers of plants and trees were aesthetically planned, so even if you just stopped and stood at the gate looking in, the vegetation led your eye from one side to the other, in a restful and relaxing way.

The next time I visited my parents in New York City, I stopped by Rat Park. A group of neighbors had organized themselves to take care of it, and the park no longer deserved its unofficial name. The trees were pruned, the ivy tamed. You could not only see the benches but actually walk up to and sit on them. Someone had installed a sculpture in one corner. You could sit down for a bit and the noise of the street would fade. I rested; I was renewed; I left the park feeling less rat race and more human. Thank you, Mr. Deacon. I get it now.

If we work to make places beautiful, we may begin to understand that we deserve beauty and that it is worth fighting for. We come to remember that a lake is not just instrumentally useful for the water and fish and other harvestable benefits, but it is spiritually valuable because of the awe and wonder it strikes in us. Conservation work is important not just for the species that can be saved but for the open space that can be enjoyed. If we spend time in beautiful and beloved places, we are inspired to believe that we are beautiful and beloved too. Perhaps this is the wisdom behind the observation of Sabbath: we should take time to rest and enjoy the goodness of God's creation. When our needs for love and belonging are unmet, we hurry through our lives and do not take time to enjoy life. Maybe we do not know how to stop worrying and hurrying, or maybe we do not even feel we deserve a day of rest and enjoyment. That rush is good for someone's bottom line, of course, but it is not ultimately good for us. Meanwhile, God calls to us from the trees and rocks and lakes and sky: Come and rest awhile! Come and take a Sabbath, a rest, a re-creation. Feel yourself part of the world, and know you are my beloved child.

Floating with Fireflies

We are all really very blessed because of where we live. Redwood trees, the Pacific Ocean, lakes, so many things. I'm in a landlocked state right now (at college), it's boring AF.

—MELVIE, nineteen

I was a city kid. Now, the youth that I minister to, in the hills of Oakland, are urban enough. Yes, they take buses and trains and appreciate good graffiti art and serve at soup kitchens. Still, because of the size and proximity of the parks around us and the closeness of the ocean, they really identify more as nature kids. Many of them have their own backyards and a surprising number keep a garden just for fun. I grew up near Central Park, which is constantly groomed by a large staff of professional gardeners. Here, they have a regional park system bigger than Manhattan itself, featuring long wilderness hikes, pastures where cattle graze, and signs warning about mountain lions. Yes, they have the usual teenage freak-out moment when we pass out of cell phone reception into wilderness (to be honest, so do I), but they are used to it.

My early experiences as a camp counselor helped me know how to ease a city kid into the country, with the lessons about ticks and deer, the canoe safety drills, and the quiet times in nature, teaching them to trust the world around them. But as a pastor to Oakland youth, I was surprised to learn I have to call on the opposite skills as we take these nature kids on more urban trips.

We arrived in New York City via Newark Airport, ready for a week of service and learning at Broadway Presbyterian Church. We took a very civilized shuttle bus from the airport, where everyone had their own seat. So the transition started slowly. They pressed their phones against the window for shots of the skyline. But when we arrived in Times Square to catch a subway uptown, their wide-eyed wonder became more like scrambled panic. Each person had to lug their own suitcase through a block or two of pressing crowds, get through a subway turnstile, and follow us through more crowds onto a subway platform. We had barely counted off to be sure the whole group was there when a train pulled up, mostly full already, and we split the group, sending half with me and half with Jim. Yes, I told them, we can get on this train, and they looked at me with disbelief. Yes, go ahead and pack in like sardines. Stand straddling your suitcase. You can put your arm between these two strangers to grab the pole. Grace looked over at me and mouthed "I love this so much" as we screeched out of the station—she had been NYC dreaming for a while—but the others looked around with alarm as they smelled the body odors and felt the elbow jabs of their neighbors whenever the train started or stopped.

Over the next few days, we all put miles on our walking shoes. We worked hard in the "four-star soup kitchen," hopping to attention whenever the chef demanded something of his volunteer crew. We sweated hard out on Staten Island where they were still (six years later!) doing the work of recovery from Hurricane Sandy. We played hard, too, jumping back on the subways whenever we had time for tourist pilgrimages to the Stonewall Inn, the UN, Central Park. On the Fourth of July, we joined throngs of humanity packed onto a highway as tightly as in any rush-hour subway. We sat on hot pavement for hours awaiting the fireworks over the East River. The youth passed the time playing the question game "Would you rather" and I overheard someone pose the question, "Would you rather be here, now, or in hell?" Grace and a few other city-obsessed people thought people-watching in these crowds was absolute heaven, but Naz put her earbuds in and her head down, drawing in her sketchbook to survive the crush. Even going out for dinner was not necessarily relaxing; New York restaurants are tinier and far more crowded than Californians are used to. Every night when we debriefed, I asked about their feet, their blisters, their energy levels, but I also watched their shoulders for tension, which was often high. Every time I looked at Mimi, I got a teeth-bared smile, an "I'm okay" grimace.

On the morning of the Fourth, though, we broke our routine. The soup kitchen service was stripped down to hot dogs and shaved ice, served on the sidewalk, which took only a few people to manage. So I asked for volunteers to head up to the roof garden. Curious, Mimi and Fred and Melvie came up. It was a steep stair climb and required some rail holding, confidence, and athleticism to get to the top of this hundred-year-old church building, about four stories high, just a bit higher than the trees nearby. Once you clambered through a packed storage space and emerged onto the roof, you could see the tiniest garden ever. The four raised garden beds could have fit comfortably in my California bedroom. Fred took the measure of this little garden and said, "Four of us? We can do this in ten minutes."

Melvie squealed, "Dandelions!" She squealed even more enthusiastically when I told her we could pull them and bring them downstairs to feed to the nursery school's bunny rabbit.

Mimi said nothing, as she dug her nose into the parsley and took a deep breath.

The garden was small, but it was enough. Here were thickly planted herbs growing for the soup kitchen downstairs, and a bunch of weeds for us to pull, and butterflies flying in and around the flowers of the parsley bolting to seed, and the sweet smell of topsoil that had been carried, bag by bag, up the ancient stairs to make this garden possible. It was a tiny miracle.

We worked for more than Fred's prophesied ten minutes . . . perhaps not much longer, but we all got lost in the weeds a bit. We trimmed herbs and pulled weeds and wrapped stacks of greens in newspaper to take downstairs: dandelions for the rabbit, herbs for the kitchen, weeds for the compost bin. We got into the little rhythm of it, letting our eyes catch the subtle differences between weed and herb, letting our hands guide us through the small thickets of greenery, letting our breath out. When we were done, Mimi shouldered the little stack of weeds and smiled.

It was the first true smile I had seen from her all week, shoulders loose again and eyes bright. She said later, "New York is a stressful city. There's so much going on and you're in the middle of so much, but the little garden was secluded and away and high up, so I found solace in that."

We saw a similar thing on the last night of the trip, when we went out to hear a swing band in a tiny park. The dancers of the group slipped straight into their happy place, but that left some nondancing folk on the sidelines, as tightly wound and crowd oppressed as ever. We were out, though, in a park at night, and it did not take long for those who were uninterested in dancing to notice what was blinking in the bushes around us. Fireflies! An eastern US treat, an entomological pleasure that never made it past the Rockies to California. Naz and Sam ran around catching fireflies and taking photos of them. They disappeared into a reverie of studying, playing, leaping, catching, and photographing; their own, unchoreographed dance to the rhythm of their tiny blinking partners. They shook off the anxiety of big-city living and fell out of time into the sheer joy of these fascinating creatures. We had to pull them away when it was time to go.

"It doesn't have to be the blue iris," Mary Oliver writes. It could be a box of dirt on a rooftop or a firefly; a radish or the irrepressible dandelions. Just pay attention; just lie back and let yourself float. We need nature, need it for our health and our sanity and our sense of connection to the One who created it. Creation is rich with blessings for us. And these blessings are not restricted to the highest mountain, the clearest sea, or the rarest flower. Taste and see, the Bible says, use all your senses. The Lord is good. The world is good, too, even in its brokenness, in its brutal concrete wrapping, in its frightful rush and screech and noise. This is the world "God so loved," and She does not withhold that lavish love from you. See the goodness of the earth and feel your own belovedness lift you to float on the surface of God's immeasurably deep goodness.

Part Three

STEADYING OUR STROKES

You don't have to choose it over and over again; it's not a constant sacrifice. Once you get used to it, it's part of the fabric of your existence. Like if you were swimming you wouldn't have to always tell yourself "I'm swimming"; you would just do it.

—LUCIE, twenty-one, on veganism

The second spiritual need is about reaching a destination. We choose where we are swimming to and set our eyes on that goal. There are two ways to keep ourselves steady: by constantly checking for a landmark on the horizon and by making sure our strokes are not lopsided. For many years I happily swam lopsided toward no goals whatsoever, but when I enrolled in lifeguard training class in high school, I learned that my swimming consistently dragged to the left. My right shoulder was a little less flexible and so my strokes were stronger on the other side. Without constant self-correction, I would end up headed toward the wrong side of the pool. Our coach gave me stretches to even my body out, but most of all he emphasized keeping my eyes on the prize (or the mock-drowning classmate I had to reach in however many seconds).

The coach picked at us for little things too. Were our legs out of rhythm with our arms? Were we swimming with splayed fingers instead of cupped hands? A waste of energy, he said. (Times have changed, and science now says we should have a small finger splay for more hydrodynamic efficiency. I learned the old-school way.) But all these corrections were in service of the goal: get to the swimmer in distress.

Spiritually speaking, steadying our strokes is about choosing a direction and not wasting energy as we head toward the goal. It is about having a clear sense of mission, God's calling on our life. We use big-picture thinking, setting big goals as landmarks to head toward, as well as getting into the details and developing daily habits that keep us aligned. Steadying our strokes is about knowing who God calls us to be and how to live that out.

We may create rules: "I don't eat meat," or "I'll only invest in funds that are divested from fossil fuels," or "I only fly for family." Or we may dispense with such hard-and-fast rules while remembering to regularly audit ourselves and our carbon footprint. Above all, we try to keep things in perspective: doing all we can do personally while recognizing that our most important work is collective.

We were in a video meeting with youth and college students over winter break, in early 2021, when eleventh-grade Olivia dropped the bombshell. "I'm not vegan anymore, you guys." I saw jaws drop in their little video squares as people leaned in toward the camera to make their astonishment plain.

"Well, it just happened with quarantine and everything. I was really trying in the beginning. Quarantine came around and I was just, being at home, like . . . I don't know why, but it just happened. I was really struggling."

Heads nodded around the screen.

"This has been such a hard year," Debbie put in. "It's important to be gentle with yourself and just do what you can." Debbie, adult advisor extraordinaire, is familiar with everyone's dietary needs and decisions, as she runs the youth group kitchen on retreats and trips. She has always been patient and flexible, even when people announced new food restrictions right before a trip.

"I'm okay with it," Olivia replied. "Sad, but not upset. I mean, I wish I was as inspirational as Justine or something but . . ."

A sideways grin came across Justine's face, and Melvie couldn't help herself. She was participating from her college apartment's kitchen while prepping dinner, and she rushed over to her laptop, spatula in hand, to spill the beans. "Justine is not vegan either, you guys!"

"*What?*" Jaws dropped again.

"Yeah, I'm not vegan anymore," Justine said, laughing. "Since, I don't know, early in quarantine." Faces tilted toward cameras to register our astonishment. Mimi threw her hands up so dramatically it looked like she might tip her chair over.

Justine had been the first of the group to go vegan, three or four years earlier. She took it seriously as an ethical and ecological commitment. She was always ready to offer a vegan recipe, and she coached others without getting pushy. She had made it through a semester and a half at college, faithfully eating whatever vegan options were available in the cafeteria, before quarantine landed her back home again, cooking with her family.

"Oh, my God, both of us," Olivia said. "Wow."

"I've just been kind of figuring out a balance," Justine said. "I felt a little bit trapped and I wanted to see what it was like . . . not to let myself go but just to realize I'm not going to solve the world's problems all on my own. I'm still vegetarian but not vegan."

"Well, okay, I'm not anything," Olivia said, tossing her hands up. "I'm an omnivore. But I'm not upset about it. I try to eat one totally plant-based meal a day. I heard that reducing your carbon footprint for one meal a day is like saving enough emissions to drive from one coast to another every year, so I try to do that." Heads nodded and thumbs-up reactions lit up the screen.

She went on, "Like, of course, being vegan is amazing if you can do it. But if you are not able to do it for any reason, financial or pandemic or you just have too much going on, you don't need to be super upset about that, because there are lots of bigger things like the corporations that we should be hassling to change so that my children can . . . well, live." She shrugged comedically. "I mean, it would be nice."

"Yes!" I jumped in, inspired. "It's this false religion, like if you never do a bad thing the world will be okay—but it's not true. If we're spending all our energy worrying about ourselves, that's a total distraction."

Mimi wanted to comment. "Yeah, a lot of people say stuff like that. It seems to be, like, people work in extremes. Like either you're vegan or you eat a lot of meat. Like there's nothing in the middle." Heads nodded.

"And something really funny is . . . well . . ." Mimi leaned into the drama of the moment. "I always held Olivia and Justine up, like *they're the vegan people*," she said, hands and voice rising to convey the glowing, saintly status of her peers. "But now I am trying to eat less meat and I *always* ate meat. Shit is just upside down now!"

Everyone burst into laughter again.

"But people be saying these extreme things, and we all know it doesn't work," Mimi continued, sure of herself and her decision. "Being vegan isn't going to solve all our problems. I decided if I could take a small step and just eat less meat, that's a lot less pressure."

"There's hard-core vegans and then people who completely trash on vegans," Melvie said. "I notice that." She pointed at the camera with her spoon for emphasis: I'm watching you.

"It's not worth the pressure to be extreme," Justine said. "Even though I'm mostly eating vegan, and I have all my vegan habits, I'm not an actual vegan anymore, but it helps to know I've influenced other people. It's about making small changes but also knowing that it's okay to not be perfect."

"Quarantine gave me new perspective," Olivia said. "You being perfect in the world is not going to make the world a perfect place."

Conversation moved on from there to other topics. But Debbie and I talked later and agreed: How wonderful it is to watch them working these things out together. How fascinating to see them take turns inspiring one another. And for our parts, we are still working on our collection of crowd-friendly, low-carbon, vegan recipes for the youth—even if nobody ends up being "an actual vegan."

Chapter 10

Back to the Stars

You could be trying to help the ecosystem . . . but not know how easy it is to disrupt it.

—DEAN, fourteen

I brought beads to youth group one week. I taught the teenagers how to make Anglican-style prayer beads and how you can pull them through your fingers one by one, saying a word or prayer for each one. I told them this is a nice way to pray if you are not good at being silent. You do not have to empty your mind, just focus it as you repeat the prayer or word you chose for each bead. I told them the practice is not about "staying centered" but about "returning to center," bringing your mind back over and over again to hold on to what is good.

I mean, they *might* pray with them. I am always filled with doubt about things like this. I would have used prayer beads when I was sixteen, but my perspective on what works for teenagers is totally skewed because I was such a religious teenager. I still have a hard time guessing what is going to work for more average young people, those who do *not* copy out Scriptures in Hebrew calligraphy for fun on the weekends. Despite my doubts, the beading project went well. They gathered around the bead boxes on the floor like fish at feeding time, wriggling around one another, hands darting in one at a time to take a few more beads out of the boxes. By the end of the night, each of them had a unique set of prayer beads. I told myself if they do not use them to pray with, perhaps at least the beads will hang on a keychain and remind them of church. . . . And maybe one day someone will tell me they have been using the prayer beads ever since, and all my pastoral self-doubt will be vanquished. The lesson is for me too—it is not about staying centered but returning to center.

Anyway, our hands were busy with this project. And as we sat on the floor stringing beads together, I told them the starfish parable, the story of how I went walking on the beach one day when there was a really, really low tide.

The tide pools were dry; the whole beach was dry. The water was low and still retreating . . . It was so low that the waves were tiny ripples, farther away from the dunes than you'd ever seen. The sand by the water was packed hard, and you could smell all this drying seaweed. Everywhere you could see drying, dying creatures . . . the starfish.

"They aren't called starfish, though," said Dean.
"Yeah, sea stars!" said Melvie with enthusiasm.
Yes, they were correct.

"Starfish are sea stars. Because stars aren't classified as fish—no more than jellies are," Dean said.

"Jellies?" from Julia.

"You know, jellyfish, but they aren't actually fish either," Fred put in.

He was right. Go to the Monterey Bay Aquarium once or twice, and you start to feel really smart about a few things (at least stars and jellies). Also, you can (forevermore) confidently identify an ocean sunfish, which is a fish, though it is the oddest fish you have ever seen. Sam says, "It's a fish, but it's a pancake too." Okay, well, back to the stars. (Remember, the practice is not remaining centered—the practice is returning to center.)

That evening with a low, low tide I was walking on the beach . . .

"Wait—did this story really happen to you?" Julia needed to know.

I smiled. "No. You got me there. But it's a story that was passed on to me this way, so I tell it this way: I walked down the beach and I saw hundreds of sea stars. They shone in the morning sun, they wriggled their legs, but they weren't moving enough. They were stranded . . . they were going to die. I took one up and threw it into the waves, but there were ten more just there. And then another ten. I kept walking, hoping that I'd see the end of it, but it was endless. I was feeling upset, because there was so much death on the beach."

"Like that day in Monterey," put in Sam, without lifting her head from her beads.

"*That day!*" Melvie sputtered, putting her beads down to gesture wildly with wide-open hands. "It was so bad! We found a dead *sunfish*, people." That was a difficult day. Beached creatures were in various stages of decomposition—seals, fish, birds, crabs. Somehow the currents worked to carry many aquatic corpses to a final resting place on this beach by Elkhorn Slough. But we knew many had died because of the plastic in their stomachs. Thus the importance of the beach cleanup. Anyway, back to the stars.

> *I walked down the beach, feeling lost around so much suffering. Would some of them make it? How long can a sea star live without water? Could I have made a difference if I had brought a bucket? I wished I could bring the waterline back up, like some kind of ocean witch.*
>
> *Farther down the beach, I climbed over a jetty. It was thick with mussels, and it was stranded all the way out of the water. As I climbed down the other side and looked down the beach, through the shining rainbow-colored light, I saw someone there. She was stooping down, picking something up, throwing it into the sea. I came closer. She kept moving. Stooping, lifting a star, disking like a Frisbee, sending them spinning into the waves. She looked at me and smiled. I kicked the sand a bit and looked around awkwardly. "Spring tide," I said.*

"What does that mean?" asked Sam, ever the collector of vocabulary words. It means the lowest of low tides—and the highest of high tides, the times when they are extreme.

"Which happens when the sun and moon line up across from each other," said Dean. That's true. Also, there is a point in the year when the sun is closer to the earth and the tides are even more extreme then.

"January," said Fred, who is a fount of knowledge on this topic, mainly because his mother is an oceanographer.

"So the spring tide doesn't actually happen in the spring?"

I was glad I had looked this up. There is a spring tide every month, but the most extreme spring tides are in January—Fred was right. Back to the stars.

I said, "Spring tide," and she said yes and turned back to squat and pick another up.

—the process is not to remain centered but to return to center—

Yes, she said, the lowest this year. I watched her throw another few. "There are so many, though." I said, "You can't possibly make a difference." She squatted and took a big one up, turned, and threw left-handed. It landed with a soft splunk in the water. "It made a difference to that one," she said.

Mac burst into a volley of what would probably have been curses if he were not at youth group; instead, they were sounds of frustration. His entire set of beads had just slipped off the string. The older girls rushed to console him. An adult advisor, sitting next to him, assured him that she also hated beading. "It's okay, you've got all your beads right here, just try again."

"But did you know?" Dean had a fact to share. "A scientist named Robert Paine did an experiment on that in 1963, where they put the sea stars back in the water instead of letting them die on the beach. And it wasn't a good thing. Because they ate all the snails, and the ecosystem was disrupted."

God, these teenagers are smart. I am out of my depth. I really did not expect Dean's fact to come up today and ruin my inspirational story time, but I know his point is true. Ecosystems are fragile. Sometimes we are distressed by death, but if we step in too quickly to relieve our distress, we might be acting emotionally without good evidence and curing one problem by causing another.

"That's what happened when people killed so many otters that there was nothing there to eat the sea urchins, and the urchins ate all the kelp, and the kelp forests disappeared," Melvie remembered. We had that lesson told to us several times on our mission trip.

"No, my story is the opposite," Dean said, emphatic. "He wasn't hunting anything. He was trying to help the ecosystem. He just didn't know how easy it was to disrupt it."

"Yeah, we need to save the otters," Sam agreed, "they're endangered. But maybe don't try to save the sea stars unless you literally know how many sea stars there are supposed to be."

"It's like when they fought forest fires by just putting all the fires out, and then they realized that, no, the forest needs to burn sometimes," Naz contributed.

"I wonder how we know what to do," Melyssa put out in a bid for further exploration of Dean's theme. "We know that hunting the otters isn't a good thing, but what if us trying to help isn't really helping the ecosystem?"

"Well," Olivia said, "I feel like the whole ocean is struggling right now, like all the ecosystems are having a hard time with climate change, and the water is warming and getting more acid. . . ."

"I thought it was less acid?" asked Dean.

"No, it's more acid." Sam was sure.

"Anyway, so like the whole ecosystem is struggling, so maybe because of that, it is a good thing to keep the sea stars from dying and throw them back in again," Olivia finished.

"Yeah, I read that," Sam remembered. "The sea stars *are* definitely dying because of the warmer water these days. So I guess you should actually help save as many as you can."

I did not know what to say. This starfish story was written in the 1970s. People might not have known so much about ecosystem balance back then; the experiment Dean mentioned might not have been well known. I could not believe how complicated this story had become; it had seemed simple when I prepared the lesson. I tried desperately to hold on to my plan and teach them what *I* had learned:

"Well, I think the story works if you're thinking about something that's not part of an ecosystem. Like if you think about collecting plastic trash or something. You can't clean up all the plastic in the ocean, but you can help one piece at a time."

"Yeah, plastic trash is *the worst*. Always pick it up," said Melvie.

But inwardly I was daunted. Maybe if you have a clear cause, then this story works, because it teaches you basically to not give up. I mean, that is what it taught me. Is that what it teaches the youth group? Or does this story need to turn into a parable about the dangers of sentimental do-good-ism? Is this a story of the older generation, who believe everything will just be okay if you do a nice thing every once in a while? What really *is* the moral of this story?

"*Noooooooooooooooooooooo!*" Mac tipped over into the fetal position. He had strung his entire set of beads over again from the beginning, only to have them all slip out when he tried to make a knot. This time people laughed. Everyone offered to help or console. Grimly, he started again.

"Can I tell one more part of the story, though?" I asked, trying to restart the conversation on my original terms. "It actually does go on." They nodded.

So I went back home that day feeling like the person who was throwing stars back into the water had it right and I had it wrong somehow, but I couldn't quite get my mind around the sheer amount of death and dying all around me, and I felt embarrassed and I didn't want to go back. But then I thought this is really what life is about—doing what you can in the face of enormous suffering. And so the next morning, I went out and I saw the star thrower was there again. And this time I joined her. And I wondered if this was what all of life was—if on the edge of the universe somewhere, God had thrown our sun, our solar system, our galaxy out to live, just like us throwing a star into the ocean.

"Mmm, that's a nice ending," Melvie sighed.

Others nodded vaguely. Maybe they had stopped paying attention when it got a little moralizing. I felt sure I had lost half of them.

"Do you know why this couldn't have been a real story Talitha actually experienced, though?" Sam raised her head brightly, ready to entertain.

"I knew it wasn't her, too, because I heard the story from someone else."

"I saw a card in the Hallmark store with this story on it."

"Right, but do you know why it *couldn't* actually be Talitha?"

"Okay, tell us why."

"Because if Talitha was in this story," Sam said, drawing it out for her audience, "she'd be the one throwing the stars back, not the one walking on the beach feeling all emo about it."

"Ha!"

"Right? Not in a million years would Talitha actually be the emo one."

"Aww, that's sweet," I said, hugging that warm affirmation to myself, though it seemed like a little bit of a misfit at the moment. I may have been playing the role of a hopeful activist, but inside, I was kind of a mess. I felt daunted and sobered by the science the youth had brought to what I thought was an uncomplicated story about not giving up.

"Thanks, Sam. But . . . I hope I wouldn't accidentally disturb an ecosystem." They all laughed.

I could disturb an ecosystem, though. I could be disturbing it right now. Perhaps not a literal one, but I know I have a profound effect on the spiritual lives of these young people, and I could make mistakes. I could be leading them in the wrong direction. For a long time, I had focused on how they should have hope and believe in a positive future, hold on to the possibility that we would turn it all around and have a clean, cool, healthy earth like God intended. Then the young Swedish activist Greta Thunberg roared into all our lives, and the first thing I remember her saying was, "Don't give me hope. I don't want your hope. I want you to panic. I want you to act like your house is on fire." This convicted me deeply, and I repented. I started cutting myself off when I found myself midway into this kind of "let's have hope" exercise. I started thinking maybe the kids need to panic. Maybe I do too.

We have all encountered the cutting accusation that religion—in general—can be an opiate, a sedative, a spiritual bypass, something that reduces your pain just enough to stop your activism. This critique holds when religion is shallow: when it gives us a little hope, enough to pray and feel better, but not enough to actually stand up and become the answer to our prayers. A shallow environmentalism can be the same kind of opiate: enough to pick up a few pieces of trash and feel better, but not enough to hit the streets and demand real and lasting change. A deep faith (like a deep environmentalism) will lead to confrontation and challenge.

The young people in my church have their own spiritual ecosystems, balanced delicately between hope and fear. More than teaching them, my job is to help them tend these ecosystems. My work is equipping them with tools for their spiritual lives, giving them some beads and some faith to hold on to, and seeing and honoring their work. I can point out when they are headed in the right direction and when they are swimming lopsided.

Sometimes, though, I find myself feeling paralyzed by the science of it all when my lesson plans veer off course and I cannot get back to center. How *do* you keep an ecosystem balanced? I really do not know enough. How many sea otters are needed to keep a population of urchins in check? How much should an urchin population fluctuate in, say, a ten-year period? What population of otters is sustainable enough to delist them from endangered status? How often does a forest need a big fire? When is a dead sunfish a tragedy, and when is it part of the circle of life? Which species need to be picked up off the beaches, and which should be left as food for the gulls?

I wonder what kind of spiritual help I should be giving these young people. I long for some scientific answers, theories, data. I just do not know enough. Are there purer sources of hope available, a hope that is uncontaminated by naïveté? What is the proper ratio of hope to panic, or does the ratio depend on global temperature averages? What is the boiling point of hypocrisy? At what precise depth does religion transform from an opiate to a catalyst? How much hope is too little? Where are we going? And will the youth ever use the prayer beads?

Chapter 11

Trying to Be Sustainable

We're trying to be sustainable but all the major companies have their hands in so many things. It's really hard to buy anything that is actually *genuinely* sustainable. That's a big problem when you want to do something that's easy, or simple to do, but even just trying to change what you buy is really hard.

—MIMI, nineteen

The second spiritual need—the one that often comes up powerfully during the teen years—is the need for meaning and direction. We long to know what is important in life, which way we should go, what to do next. When this need is unfilled, and the need is deep, we become confused and unsure, even paralyzed with indecision. Then we come to church wanting someone to guide us: we would like to fall in line and have someone else make decisions. But in fact, the better way, the way that will lead to growth and transformation, is for each of us to look inward and clarify our values. A good guide through this process will not tell us what to do but will listen and reflect our core values back to us. Values are so much more helpful when they are ours by choice—not someone else's choice.

The second spiritual need is about finding meaning in the meaningless swirl of stuff around us. We look at the shore and pick out one tree or post as our goal. We name the stuff that matters and jettison whatever does not. And we learn to keep ourselves moving with sure strokes toward our goal.

If someone comes to your church longing for meaning and direction, they could be coming from a number of different angles. Maybe something came into their life—a new diagnosis or a failure at school—and it threw some complex decisions in their path, questions seeking answers. They may be stuck in a swirl where a river divides, currents pulling them back and forth, exhausted with indecision. But sometimes the questions are not so clear, and this need emerges as a fog of boredom; why not just tread water and stay where you are?

In light of the climate crisis, many young people are finding themselves in deep need of direction, like the Hebrew people, postexodus, wandering in the desert. They want to serve, to rescue, to help—but they do not know where or how. They wish for a modern Moses who could give them ten clear commandments and guarantee that following those commandments would lead them to the promised land.

My generation lived by three ecological commandments: Reduce, Reuse, Recycle. Easy to remember, easy to follow: just reach into the garbage and pick out the cans. It was as simple as my first-ever lifeguard rescue. I was standing by the camp pool when a girl treading water just below me looked up, locked eyes with me, and quietly gasped "help." I dropped to my knees, reached out my arms, and pulled her small body up to sit next to me on the edge of the pool before anyone even noticed there was a rescue in process.

Today's ecological commandments are much more complex. Rethink your choices; reduce carbon use; refuse disposable plastic; reuse everything; refurbish old things; repair before you replace; repurpose creatively. Recycling no longer makes us feel good about ourselves, since we know our "recycled" goods are being shipped across the globe to so-called recyclers who do not even want the materials. The quest to follow these complicated commandments is more like the rescues they warned us about in lifeguard class: there are swimmers in distress far out in the waves, lost and barely visible. We send out a search party in hope.

Meanwhile, a kind of personalized, greenwashed materialism has arisen to enable us to navigate by simply following advertisements for consumer products. The corporations, after all, have their hands in everything, and where there is desire, there is opportunity for exploitation. So they sell us guilt-free products in an increasingly frenzied competition to be the eco-friendliest. They want to sell me dresses made of bamboo, milk delivery services in glass bottles, shoes made of recycled plastic, bars of shampoo wrapped in paper (no bottle!), and panties you can monthly bleed into and wash clean without anything to dispose of. I could spend a fortune on such tiny improvements. Spending too much energy evaluating them strikes me as a massive distraction from the main goal of cutting carbon emissions.

We get into arguments over more complicated equations seeking to reduce carbon emissions. There is a tree shading our neighbor's house that blocks the sunlight and makes them turn up the heater in the winter. Does the carbon being sequestered by the tree equalize the use of fuel needed to heat the home? A friend calculated the difference in carbon footprint between eating meat at home and driving to a restaurant for a vegan dinner, and it was close enough to be affected by the fuel efficiency of your vehicle. Which commandment do you observe first, then? Thou shalt not pollute, or Thou shall eat lower on the food chain?

These complex and competing commandments and subcommandments give us a certain angst: it is hard to know which one is important, which one is very important, and which one is *adiaphora* (Greek church-speak for "doesn't matter"). So we get exhausted trying to follow them all.

Alternatively, when we have one or two commandments down pat, we focus on them to a fault. Consider, for example, the people who get self-righteous about waste and trash. You know them, right? They carry metal straws and forks in their bags, so they never touch the uncleanness of disposable plastic items. They fish organics out of the trash to compost at home. They avert their eyes in horror from even the sight of Styrofoam. I know these people well, for I am one. I will find myself at a church not my own, and it is time for a meal, and I have forgotten my reusable water bottle at home. They are handing out bottled water with warmth and hospitality and good cheer. There I stand, caught between righteousness in the eyes of the ecological commandments and the social commitments I have made to be a gracious guest, which precludes my interrupting the dinner line with loud lectures about Nestlé.

Generally, in such situations, I silently and urgently tell myself that I am accepting the bottle out of graciousness to my hosts. I say some Hail Rachel Carsons later as penance and try not to feel too dirty from cross contamination. Jesus accused the lawyers and Pharisees (his favorite rhetorical opponents) of tithing mint, dill, and cumin—that is, making sure to measure out exactly what they owe God in the tiny amounts of herbs raised in their home gardens—while neglecting the major crops of justice, mercy, and faithfulness (Matt 23:23). If my bottled water boycott is an offering to God, I am sure its level of magnitude is closer to a teaspoon of mint than it is to a life of faithfulness.

So I dream of bigger ways to conserve: I dream of cohousing and tool libraries and public transportation and municipal compost services. Tackling bigger issues helps us not get into such a spiritual twist about one plastic bottle or straw. We do not need to stress so much over whether our fingers are in the proper (cupped or splayed) swimming position, because we know we have our eyes on the goal and are constantly self-correcting.

I spent some time looking at the top projects we need to focus on, globally, to reduce carbon in the atmosphere (a list published by Project Drawdown). It was a real buzzkill, because none of my consumer commitments were highly ranked. Electric bikes make the cut, toward the end of the list, but giving up water bottles is not even on the page. Refrigerants are a major issue. Being a renter, I have never been responsible for the purchase of a refrigerator (or even an air conditioner unit, living in mild Northern California). Everything I know about refrigerants I learned on the Drawdown website. Yes, I remembered that "CFC" stands for "something terrible," but I did not know that the chemicals that have come to replace the older CFCs, while sparing the ozone layer, now wreak havoc on carbon emissions. I filed that fact in my back brain along with the swim coach's inscrutable advice to kick upward as well as downward. It makes theoretical sense, but I cannot figure out how *I* could actually do it.

It is hard to keep a healthy perspective about our consumption and waste. What we buy and use and eat and throw away takes up a large part of our day-to-day life, and even if it is not the most important thing, we still find it catches our attention. One of my more peculiar fixations is guilt about throwing fabric away. In college I read *Woman on the Edge of Time* (by Marge Piercy). I must have missed a lot when I read it the first time; rereading it in adulthood, I was amazed by the time travel, the uterine replicators that liberated women from childbearing, the polyamorous relationship structures, and the long sessions of communal psychotherapy. But one small thing I had not forgotten: flimsies. When the main character gets taken to a celebration in the eco-utopian future, she finds that the people dress up by designing a "flimsy" garment that gets 3D printed from organic material. These garments last a day and a night, and then you throw them on the compost heap. Why spend more labor and material on something you only wear once?

The obsession with compostable fabric stayed with me whenever I bought a garment I knew I would only wear once. It stuck with me naggingly when I made my wedding dress, and I promised myself that I would eventually dye the dress to use it again. It relaxed its grip only when I made quilts of reused fabric and it tightened in a chokehold whenever I tried to throw fabric away, so I ended up with boxes full of theoretically useful fabric that I just could not throw away. I tried to release the obsession from my mind along with the rest of the apparently forgettable ideas from this utopia. But the flimsy idea was (is!) still firmly stuck in my brain. I belong, after all, to a generation who grew up on trash and recycling as the Great Ecological Issues; as a kid I read *Ranger Rick* magazines that threatened us with tales where Earth became one big trash heap spinning through space. How could I just throw fabric in the trash when I had read a utopian novel once that had compostable fabric in it? *What would Ranger Rick do?*

When I moved into the manse at Montclair Presbyterian, my fabric stash finally met its destiny. The front garden was full of hard-packed clay soil, impossible to dig into, so rather than dig down, I built up, layering fabric underneath cardboard, straw, and compost. The not-so-flimsy fabrics worked as weed cloth for a few years, and then gracefully gave up the ghost. The layers of compost decomposed with them, and the cotton all broke down under the layers. I do find bits of the original apparel, though—a scrap of polyester interfacing, a trailing piece of thread, here or there a stray button. When I find these pieces, they remind me that I did this project alone. The makers of the garments were not on the same ecological page as me, and we do not have great systems set up for fabric recycling.

I no longer fear the trash-filled planet quite so keenly; we are set on a climate course that will waste the planet in more existential ways long before we run out of room for landfills. But the vision still stays in my mind. I do not know how we get from here to there—that utopia where we can all 3D-print a compostable garment for free—but in the meantime, the act of fabric conservation calls me to mindfulness. Like a swimmer remembering to keep their fingers aligned right, I enjoy the feeling of grace and alignment that the mindfulness adds to my daily life.

> *I've noticed how environmentalism is becoming split between certain people wanting to make change and certain people needing to make change. With food deserts—not having access to fresh fruits and vegetables and stuff—that's something you need. Whereas other people just want to have less plastic and stuff. There's definitely different types of access to environmentalism. Some people are going to try to use mason jars and be reusable, and other people are like "I literally cannot afford x, y, and z; I have no choice."*
>
> —Justine, twenty

Mindfulness is not the whole of the spiritual life, but it is an important tool. Being mindful of what we do with our trash and recyclables is one kind of ecospiritual mindfulness. Remembering to look to the poorest members of society is another. Being mindful about how we talk to ourselves—scanning internally for pride out of proportion, perhaps—is an important companion to the other kinds of mindfulness. If you are going to attempt the spiritual discipline of reducing the trash you throw away, it is important to also attempt the simultaneous spiritual discipline of remembering to keep the little things in proper perspective. Plastics are a huge problem, globally speaking. But one could go entirely plastic-free and still have a huge carbon footprint (like the person who went viral for demanding a plastic-free drink cup on their international flight); your eye is on the wrong goal here. Or you could even reduce your personal carbon footprint to a minuscule amount, but unless you are also taking action to help others reduce theirs and to advocate for better policies and products, you could still be headed off in the wrong direction because you're alone.

> *They asked only one thing, that we remember the poor, which was actually what I was eager to do.*
> —Galatians 2:10

Personal environmentalism makes a compelling religion; one can compete for purity, scoring points for never touching plastic. But it does not make an inclusive religion or a compassionate one. If your eyes are set only on personal goals, you are setting out alone. If your goals are inaccessible to your neighbor who is impoverished, your potential team is much smaller. Climate activism is not a swim competition where you get points for style; it is not even one where you can get points for a personal-best time. The only thing that matters here is the rescue itself. One bold swimmer out ahead of the rest may be able to cheer and inspire us, but they will need the entire team to bring everyone back.

In the worldwide race to help and heal our climate, it seems clear that reducing carbon is the most important metric, and so we all need to keep that goal foremost in our minds. On the way to that big goal, we can find smaller, individual ways to will help the environment. We can eat less meat or meat from more sustainable sources. I will never forget the look on our (then) actual-vegan Olivia's face at a national conference where a rural youth spoke up saying he hunts and eats venison to reduce his carbon footprint. We can reduce consumption in our households, organizations, and businesses, and we can advocate for local and regional laws that make such reductions possible, affordable, and accessible to others, so as many people as possible can join this environmental rescue team. We will not get out of the climate crisis one plastic straw or water bottle at a time; being purist about such things will alienate those who do not care and irritate those who have a keener sense of the emergency. You would not exclude a swimmer from your rescue team who could swim fast but who had a stiff shoulder making them veer off to one side. No, you would encourage them, stretch with them, and keep them on track by calling them back to the goal every so often.

The second spiritual need is expressed in large and small ways, the daily and the lifetime goals. In the big picture, we meet this need with carbon counting, political action, divestment and boycott, and policy work. This is the spiritual skill of navigation, identifying a goal and setting out toward it with constant course correction. In daily life, we meet this need in the regular practice of ecological mindfulness, from what we buy to what (and how) we throw things away. This practice helps us develop muscle memory, locking us into the course we have already set.

Chapter 12

Choosing Carefully

Be careful. Choose where you put your energy.

—JILL, nineteen

When we set out for a destination together, we have to communicate about it. We have to name our destination in a way that others can follow and comprehend. Any names will do, if they function for us; but the words we choose are still important.

Nobody can pronounce my name. Talitha rhymes with Latifa. I have gotten used to having it mangled. At Starbucks, I just give a nickname: "Tahoe, like the lake." I tell children they can call me Pastor T. Or sometimes I just brace myself to laugh. But laughing off the mispronunciations is not always easy. If you get my name wrong, still I feel embarrassed. As Frederick Buchner wrote, "If you mispronounce my name I have a feeling that what you've forgotten is me."

Names for God and Jesus are important too. They tell you what to expect. I like the simple "God," which for me is nearly broad enough to encompass the mystery of God. But for others, that word is too narrow. Some like the richness of metaphorical names such as "Lighthouse" or "Lover of My Soul," while others are turned off by how specific they are. The name "Savior" is a good one, but in turn, it can be problematic. Naming the divine as "Savior" begs the question—when will God save us, and how? Will the Savior save us from climate change? What about just saving me from my dreaded calculus exam? Will the Savior rescue me from cancer? Or is that rescue in the hands of my oncologist?

As we struggle with the second spiritual need, looking for meaning and direction, we will need to identify our landmarks, especially those with cosmic significance. That means coming up with our own names for the divine, whether as mild as adding a descriptor, such as "Gardening God," or as radical as saying "God is change," as in Octavia Butler's dystopian parables. We need this theological freedom to change, to rename, to respond to what is happening as the environment around us changes.

Names are important for stories too, and especially for sacred stories. The titles interpret the story for us: who the central character is or what the moral is. Take a familiar one: the Parable of the Prodigal Son. The same passage could also be titled "The Lost Son" or "The Forgiving Father." Or, depending on whom you relate to in the story, "The Parable of the Stupid Younger Brother." (Older siblings everywhere know what I'm talking about.) However, whenever a teacher introduces it as "The Parable of the Prodigal Son," we limit its focus and tell listeners ahead of time who the story is *about*.

It can be extra damaging if someone authoritatively shuts off an avenue of interpretation that could have brought us good news we needed. It stunts our spiritual growth when someone declares, "The answer is Jesus," and leaves out the possibility that the Good Shepherd, for you, could actually have the same name as your doctor or nurse.

In our church's Godly Play rooms, the parables are told using materials in gold-painted wooden boxes with a little colored dot on the side. When we take parables to the hospital, we fill four-inch gold boxes from the party-favor store with miniature versions of the same felt and paper pieces, adapting the classroom-size story pieces to fit on a child's bed. I know these stories as the Good Shepherd, the Sower, the Good Samaritan, the Pearl of Great Price, and the Mustard Seed, but I keep those names in my head and off the box. As at church, the box is not labeled with words, just a little dab of color to help me tell them apart. If the child asks what the story is "about" I say, "I don't know, but when I'm done telling the story, maybe you can tell me what it's about, for you."

The grown-ups in the church could take some lessons from our Sunday school classroom. Bible publishers could take note too. I found the quote from Luke 18:17, where Jesus threatens "Remember this! Whoever does not receive the Kingdom of God like a child will never enter it" (GNT). written up under the polite heading "Jesus Blesses Little Children." How about "Jesus Rebukes the Grown-Up Gatekeepers"? The publishers were thinking about gentle Jesus, meek and mild; maybe they forgot he was also the wild man who turned over tables in the temple.

Once I was telling a story to a patient and her brother, both under the age of eight, cuddled up together in the hospital bed. Their pious parents hovered nearby and prompted them: "Oh, we know who the Good Shepherd is, don't we?"

"He's a good person," the brother replied, and I nodded gravely in affirmation.

"Don't you remember his name?" the mother asked, leadingly.

"No," the brother replied, cocking his head.

I should have jumped in with my line: "We didn't learn the Good Shepherd's name in this story. And there are no right answers here . . ." But I was not quick enough.

"J . . . J . . . J . . ." prompted Mom.

"Joseph!" crowed the sister triumphantly. Dad snorted a little laugh, but I didn't think it was funny at all.

"No, Joseph had a baby . . . remember, Mary and Joseph had baby . . . baby J . . . baby J . . . J . . . J . . ."

"Jesus," she said, with chilled enthusiasm: she had just gotten schooled.

In another hospital room, just down the hall, an older boy said he thought the Good Shepherd was probably Saint Jude, and he touched the medallion his grandmother had given him for protection through his medical treatments.

A colleague of mine, Di Pagel, was in the Godly Play classroom on the day a fifth grader who'd been attending weekly Sunday school for years had an epiphany. He looked back and forth from one story to another on the shelf in the classroom.

His eyes bugged out with holy wonder and he could not contain himself.

"Di!" he sputtered urgently, "Di!"

"What is it, dear?"

"Di, I think . . . I think the Good Shepherd is *Jesus!*"

That moment was as precious as gold. Because it was *his* epiphany. As far as he knew he was the only person in the world who had ever discovered it. He would never forget it.

I wished that kind of epiphany for the brother and sister in the hospital bed. And I wish it for all the children in our classes, the youth in our youth group, the college students drifting and spiritually unmoored. I wish it for all the spiritual refugees of the climate crisis, casting about for a beacon of hope.

To have our Sunday school teachers educate our children by drilling them on borrowed information seems about as useful as the Victorian waterless swimming lessons where they hoisted students in the air on ropes and had them mimic the strokes. With no sense of what they feel like in water, you will have no way to *use* the motions you have memorized. We do want children to be biblically literate enough to be able to read their Bibles and discover the place where Jesus said "I am the Good Shepherd," but we also need to leave them enough room so they can come to an epiphany that is all theirs. With our rapidly changing climate, we may need to find a totally new meaning in the text. Our needs for meaning are changing, as the world around us changes. So we need to strike the old names off our stories and be open to new names.

Here is a gold box with a light brown dot. Inside you find a long piece of light brown felt, a paper person sowing seeds, and some small paper figures: birds, rocks, thorns, soil, bushel baskets. You can use them to tell a story about a sower who went sowing seeds: they threw their seeds on the path, where the birds ate it; on the rocks and in the thorns, where it struggled to grow; and in the good soil, which yielded a great harvest.

Unfortunately, most people know immediately what this story is "about," because the Bible tells us so. It irritates me to no end that this rich and multifaceted story is summarized in moral terms . . . and in Jesus's voice no less. The Bible says that it is a parable about people's hearts: some of them are hard like the road, some shallow like the rocky soil, some distracted and confused by growing in the thorns, but never fear, there is also some good soil. Yay for good soil! So all of us who grew up in church knew that the moral of the story was to be good—to be the good soil and let God grow in you.

We need to try to unhear this ancient interpretation of the parable of the sower being about human hearts, rescuing the parable so it can speak to us today. If we read it with ecological eyes, it becomes the parable of the bad farmer. Who, when they have seeds to sow, would walk randomly, throwing seeds in every direction? Good farmers plow and measure and put all their seeds carefully into the good soil. But no, the farmer in this parable is wasteful, overgenerous, careless, stupid.

If we read with ecological eyes, we can turn this story on the Lord of Creation and say to God, "This stupid farmer is you." And forget the bit about the seeds being the word of God—the seeds are us. What kind of world is this you created, God, with seeds sown on the path and the rocks? We stare down the path of climate change, not to mention the road being walked by kids sick in the hospital, and see that God has done a lousy job planting us. We are on rocky soil, and we cannot root, and the sun is going to come up and bake us, and we will die. Why did you toss us out on the rocks like this, Lord?

I tell the parable of the sower in the hospital on the fifth floor, where kids have things like cancer and chemo and bone marrow transplants. I was tempted to skip this story, because it has the concept of death in it . . . but isn't that the whole point? Kids who do not know how long they might live need to hear stories with death in them. I smooth the felt figures out on each one's bed, and I say that the seeds on the thorny soil were trying so hard to grow, but the thorns choked them and they died. One child solemnly tells me that the seeds died and went to heaven with Jesus. Another is just happy that the birds got to eat the seeds up (he likes birds more than plants). Another child knows the moral of the story and puts on a wise preacher voice to say it: *never give up*. And later we say a prayer, and the kids' parents say they are so grateful for their child being alive, and I make a mental note to shake my fist at God later, as I leave the hospital on my bike to labor uphill. God, why not just make us all perfect? Or at least, why not plant and tend us with more attention? Why have you thrown us out like so many wildflowers to fight for our lives against the thorns?

I am no oncologist, but I know there are different kinds of cancer. Many cancers are caused by exposure to toxins or radiation. But the children are mostly suffering from the kind of cancers that come from random misfiring of DNA. It is the price we pay for having such nimble and flexible genetic material: it also makes us vulnerable to getting sick. And our fragile genes seem like so many seeds thrown out in hostile environments. Some of these seeds, sown at random, do not even come together to create a fetus that can survive to birth, and some grow into children whose lives are stopped at age five with a cancer diagnosis and a six-week hospitalization. This is the cost of living in this beautiful, diverse, harsh, and competitive world—far more like a wilderness than like a well-tended farm.

A friend of mine enrolled in a seminary that was more conservative than advertised. The semester before she dropped out, she was assigned to write a paper on how the Bible contradicts evolution. She studied science as an undergrad, so she surely was not going to fulfill her professor's expectations about the six-day Creation. Instead, she wrote the most intelligent answer I have ever heard, saying that evolution privileges the survival of the fittest, yet on the other hand, the God revealed in the Bible and particularly through Jesus Christ cares most for the poor, the vulnerable, and the oppressed. I think of her answer when tough invasive species (kudzu or human) take over and make an environment inhospitable to the more fragile species that had previously thrived there. The God I know through Jesus Christ must mourn when a tiny flower species goes extinct. And so it is only pious of me to raise my fist to the sky shouting *why*, calling my Lord to account, when a fragile five-year-old child is so threatened by cancer.

But even through this all, still I take refuge in the parable of the bad farmer, because what some might call wasteful is also the beauty of nature, the tenacious and urgent call to life. The farmer's wastefulness is like the irrepressible coast live oak between my manse and the church that drops thousands of acorns each year. The divine beauty of the bad farmer can be seen as these acorns press up into seedlings everywhere. They rarely grow past six inches tall before I throw them in the compost. Sometimes they are so well rooted in the hard clay that they cause me to curse as I yank them out. But I see the joy in them too—the oak tree is so determined to live and thrive and reproduce itself. Someday that oak will burn in a fire or topple in a flood. But when it goes down, a thousand eager volunteers will be ready: the next generation.

> *Blessed are your eyes, for they see, and your ears, for they hear. Truly I tell you, many prophets and righteous people longed to see what you see, but did not see it, and to hear what you hear, but did not hear it.*
>
> —Matthew 13:16–17

I went up to the fifth floor, stopping for an extralong hand scrub in the airlock before going into the immune-compromised unit. I looked up the new girl, cross-checking what the chaplain had written in her note to me: "Jill J. 19 years old, very spiritually aware and eager to explore. Agnostic." I sat down at the side of her bed, nothing between us but her lunch tray and the paper mask hiding my nervous smile. Jill was big (taller than me), relaxed, or perhaps just exhausted (not a single muscle in her body looked tensed), and her smooth bald head shone in the half-light of the room where she had drawn the curtains so she could sleep late. I had never encountered a patient in the children's hospital dressed in a Budweiser T-shirt before, but then again, I usually saw the kindergarten set.

The story I had brought was the parable of the sower, and I was so ready to engage this with a teenager. It was going to be so exciting to work with someone who is old enough to realize that she *is* a seed of life, currently struggling on the rocks of chemo. I could not wait to bring out all my big ideas.

Well, I told the story, moving the paper pieces around on the felt next to her lunch tray, and came to the end. For some reason I felt bashful and could not bring myself to ask her the playful prompts I give young children—"I wonder, what was the person doing when the birds came to eat up the seeds?"—and so I skipped straight to the big question.

"I wonder what seemed most important in this story."

She was ready with a smart answer: "This is a parable and Jesus told these stories to teach us a lesson, so I think the moral of the story is . . ."

—my breath held, *Please* don't *say the moral is to be good soil*—

". . . the moral is be careful. Choose where you put your energy and your effort."

Okay, at least it was not the canned answer. I thought I could still prompt her to see what it was really about: "Like choosing the best place to plant?"

She smiled as she said, "Well, you can't be upset if you put your seeds on the path and the birds eat them. Birds literally eat birdseed. You can't expect them to just leave it alone."

She was not saying the thing I wanted her to say. I tried another prompt:

"I wonder what the rocks could stand for."

"That's like the hard part in life. Where you're struggling."

I waited, smiling encouragingly. I made noises about "hmm, life is hard sometimes." I waited for her to say "This is my life: suffering." But darn it, she was not going to say it.

"And the good soil over here is like when you decide what you're doing and you do it right."

I wish I could say I pivoted and followed up with questions on her theme of decision and commitment, but I was too attached to my own precious parable interpretation. Lucky for us, though my mind was not on the right track, I still had patience and time. I gave up on prompting, sat back, and listened as she started chatting about school.

"I miss this kind of thing, you know. Like Sunday school, which I used to go to. Where we just talk about ideas and apply them to our lives. I don't get enough of it these days."

I did my autopilot chaplain thing: mm-hmmed, nodded. And she kept talking. She pushed her meal tray to the side and woke up a bit as she started talking with her hands, telling me stories. We found ourselves reliving high school band drama: "I could've been the drum major if I hadn't gotten distracted.

I tried to help a friend, but it backfired. I should've stayed in band and stayed focused. But sometimes you try to help someone, and they just take and take and take. It's over; I learned from it."

We went back to the first weeks of college, before her diagnosis: "I took four classes. I had a scholarship that said, 'You have to take twelve credits,' so I took twelve credits. But oh, my *God*, it was just too much. I was done in a couple of weeks. I just couldn't."

We talked about next year: "They said I can come back one class at a time. I'm not going to waste my time on those other classes. I want to be an accountant. So I might not even get a diploma; I can do certificates. Math classes come first."

We talked about tomorrow: "Chemo starts at midnight. First they do the premeds, and then I ask for the Benadryl and the Ativan, so I can sleep through the rest of it. But my most important job is to drink lots of water and flush the drugs back out of my system again. That's hard when you feel sick to your stomach, but I do my best. I have a mission. If I do it well, I'll go home Friday in time to see my cousins."

Her energy waning, silence fell.

She reached down and patted the story, still spread out on her bed in felt and paper. She took the little paper bushel basket and put it in the sower's arms, and smiled.

Finally, the connections rushed into my mind. I had been so distracted by my own off-course lesson plan. But she had been talking to me for twenty minutes now, and her stories were all on topic. She had summarized the story as about "choosing where you focus." And everything connected. The middle school band drama was the birds on the path, eating the seeds: she was wise enough to know it was her friend's nature to take and take, never giving back. The first weeks of college were the rocks, the struggle, the impossible attempts. Threading a path through what classes she will take and not take in the future was like the thorns—choosing carefully and making sure to clip and prune whatever isn't working. And the good soil was her clear mission: drink water, rest, more water, Benadryl, rest. Choose carefully where you spend your energy. Eyes focused on the goal.

Jill's experiences glimmered over the colored felt and paper pieces like a shining spiderweb of story. I tried to say something (anything), but I could not find words eloquent enough to honor what she had done. She was working so hard on this spiritual need: How do I know where to spend my precious little energy? Every part of this story connected to a life lesson, hard won. I mustered up a humble closing statement as I put the felt and paper pieces back in their box.

"I'm so glad I got to share this story with you. It's just . . . all so connected. Knowing what's important. And making careful choices."

Twelve steppers speak of "doing the next right thing." You do not have to know what you will be doing next year. You do not have to see all the way to your goal. But you can use your values like a beacon to stay oriented. Jill's values were illuminating baby steps, not giant leaps, but the light of her beam was as clear and focused as a lighthouse.

Chapter 13

If You Don't Pick Us Up, Who Will?

I felt really bogged down on the beach, thinking, "In a few weeks, it'll be back to litter again"—you know these negative thoughts—but even then I felt good People on the beaches were noticing what we were doing and thanking us for doing it. It felt good to think that maybe other people would be inspired to do the same.

—JUSTINE, nineteen

As we seek support in the second spiritual need, to find our beacons for meaning and direction, outsourcing can be tempting. If we could just fall in line behind a charismatic leader, we would never have to second-guess ourselves again. We could just do as we are told. We could take a place in the middle of the pack, follow the people in front of us, and forget about navigating. Taking a break from making decisions and letting someone else direct us feels so refreshing. But soon we will be lost again. We will have traveled without choosing or even knowing where we were going, and if we get separated from the group, we will not be able to find our way.

That does not mean we should strike out alone though. Falling in alongside some fellow travelers, and choosing people who can inspire us on the journey, can be extremely helpful. If they do not seek to control us or direct our behavior but just want to keep company, we can learn a lot about the journey by walking alongside them and learning from their wisdom. And so one of the most important things we can do is to identify, seek out, and fall into step for a while with those who are doing important work.

The second spiritual need is also where we deal with stamina. You have picked your goal and decided to go for it; now how do you keep your energy flowing? Whereas we learn to rest when we address the first spiritual need, here we need to muster up our energy and stay motivated. Nothing is better for this than being in the company of people who are committed to the work.

The church near Monterey, where we went for our Blue Theology mission trip, was full of such people. They were biologists and poets, conservationists and cooks, and of course they had their barista pastor who served the lattes that so perplexed and astounded us. These people did not do anything halfway. If they committed to something, they were going to do it wholeheartedly. If they hired a pastor who really liked good coffee, they were going to set up an espresso bar for him. If they committed to doing ecological mission work for the ocean, they would do it with everything they had.

They were in it for the long haul. They fully embraced the work of hosting our youth group and leading us in our mission work. On most of our previous mission trips, we had been treated kindly enough as guests but without much attention from the host congregation. Hosts might wave at us or have us stand up for some applause during the church service, and after church they would delegate someone to point out whatever needed cooking, fixing, or painting and put us to work. This trip was different. The congregation's mission focus was crystal clear, and we were at the center of it. They felt called, as a community, to help people fall in love with the ocean and its creatures. And the best way they could do this was by hosting visitors. The lattes were just the beginning. Church members came by every day to cook us pancakes, to walk us over to the aquarium, to survey the sand crab population, and to help us respond to our mission work with art and poetry. They wanted us to feel as they felt about God's beloved ocean. And as we walked alongside them that week, we found ourselves more and more focused and committed. Their stamina rubbed off on us.

Kimberly introduced herself to the youth on Tuesday. They greeted her with cool indifference in the morning, but by evening they wholly adored her. She was in the process of retiring, still full of energy and now enjoying more free time, and so she spent the whole day doing Blue Theology with us.

In the morning we worked with sand crabs. Readers will not believe that a month before the trip, Melvie said, "I can't wait to spiritually bond with sand crabs," but she did. She was really excited to have an experience with these little wriggly legged creatures. Then again, she has a pet lizard (a bearded dragon), which she loves as only a mother lizard could, so maybe I should have expected her enthusiasm.

Others were a little freaked out by the sand crabs' wriggling legs and fragile exoskeletons. Grace asked if she could maybe be the person recording measurements instead of holding sand crabs. I understood and gave her the clipboard as we got into groups of four. We were on the beach at Asilomar, a windswept expanse with patches of sunshine coming through occasionally. Well-dressed business types straggled down from the nearby convention center behind the dunes, recognizable by their lanyard name tags and their urgent cell phone conversations, but other than them, us, and a few families playing, the beach was open and empty. Kimberly made us all repeat a vow: never turn your back on the ocean. The beaches of the Atlantic where I grew up are safe enough to turn your back on, but these Pacific beaches are subject to "sneaker waves" that can sweep people out to sea with no warning. Thus vowed and equipped with our scoop tubes, mesh bags, and clipboards, we started collecting sand crabs.

Sand crabs are a sentinel species, like the canary in the mine. The health of the sand crabs, that is, tells us about the health of the local ecosystem. This is not only because they are very sensitive to small changes but also because they are deeply interconnected to other species: those they feed on and those that feed on them. If something hurts another part of the ecosystem, it is sure to also hurt the sand crabs. So a huge sand crab monitoring project, taking place over many years and many beaches, has been engaging citizen-scientists like our amateur group to keep an eye on the ecosystem via sand crabs. Each group was to take ten scoops of sand, measured out in stride lengths from the "swash zone" where waves break and striding uphill toward drier sand. We put each scoop in a mesh bag that the crabs could not escape and then went through each bag, counting, sizing, and sexing the sand crabs.

The little crabs ("recruits") are hard to tell apart, but when they are mature you can visually tell a male from a female by pulling down on its tail, not that this is an easy task! We had a couple of false starts, not confident enough to pull the tail aside, worried we would hurt the crabs, and really not sure what we were looking for, so we called Kimberly over for sex-checking. She was patient and enthusiastic, as though sex-checking sand crabs was the most delightful task in the world. Finally, we turned up a few females with bright orange eggs (we called them preggers, though they are technically not pregnant because they carry their offspring outside their body), and from then on, we were quite clear who was who. In our group I would hold the crab, Nellie would use a small stick to pull down its tail, and Justine would swoop in with the ruler to measure, head to tail. Grace stood by, clipboard in hand, and wrote down the numbers.

By the end of the hour and a half it took us to measure several hundred of the sea creatures, our group was feeling crabby. We had lost the joy with which we had crowed over our first pregger females, lost that joy somewhere in a swarm of tiny recruits that would not stay still long enough for us to find out if they were four or five millimeters each. Even Melvie did not really want to see any more sand crabs. But Kimberly was still in the flow, delighted by the work we had done, looking at each clipboard with great interest and congratulating each group for the great numbers we had gotten. The sand crab population seemed healthy, at least on this beach, and Kimberly was as happy as a grandmother who checks on the babies and finds all is well. We marveled at her.

That afternoon Kimberly took us to do a beach cleanup, part of an organized effort spanning many years and many beaches. We drove to Monterey, parked by a pier, and looked down at a beach that was just a few blocks long. Kimberly would be running some errands but would meet us again in an hour or so. She cautioned us not to tire ourselves out.

"Someone should set a timer for a half hour. Each group can go out, cleaning as you go, for a half hour, then come back, cleaning as you go."

"A half hour?" Mimi muttered to me. "This place is tiny." I agreed, thinking Kimberly was just being extra nice. We would have no trouble conquering this beach.

"*We got this!*" yelled Fred, fist in the air, and everyone nodded. But we did not know how much trash could be hiding in plain sight.

As it turned out, an hour was not nearly enough. It took us ten minutes to get twenty feet down the beach. There were rocky sections with cigarette butts tucked in every imaginable corner. We started cursing under our breath. Our group did not even make it down to the waterline in our hour of work. We found vodka bottles, fast food containers, straws, crayons, a long plastic ribbon that looked exactly like seaweed, and the shells of fireworks. Some trash could be grouped and attributed to a single source, like the 134 crayons that must have been handed out to keep children busy at a beachside restaurant. Matching plastic chocolate wrappers in a bunch of different locations made us suspect that Ghirardelli was giving out free samples up the block. We had never felt angry about free samples before.

We found the evidence of human carelessness and the testimony of human desperation. We found a nest of long-abandoned and weather-ruined supplies that must have belonged to people who were homeless, including a sign, designed for use on the hitchhiking route, saying, "If you don't pick us up, who will?" We took that cardboard message board as our sermon for the day.

We were deeply upset by the time we left the beach. Disappointment was thick in the air; long gone were our fantasies of being ecological saviors. We had spent a whole hour, in two teams, with special equipment like long-handled grabbers to make things easier to reach. We had been systematic and we worked our butts off. And we barely made a dent in the situation. We had decided not to even begin cleaning up the section of old concrete carpeted with broken glass. There was just no way to finish this job. Kimberly had dropped us off in the middle of a simply unending task.

I tried my best to cheer the group up, but I could barely cheer myself. My old millennial back was sore, and my soul felt contaminated. I had picked up and discarded a Big Gulp full of human piss. So when Kimberly came cheerfully back to meet us, I was happy to hand the pastoring over to her.

Kimberly assembled the group and asked them what they had found. They recited the litany of trash, from maddening to saddening. They vented their realizations too, along with policy proposals for biodegradable chocolate wrappers and cigarette filters. She received it all with grace and gratitude, not letting the sadness or the anger overwhelm her even as she took it in. She affirmed our learnings: yes, human poverty and ecological degradation are intertwined. Yes, policies about biodegradability would make a difference. Yes, these disposable crayon sets are ridiculous. And she kept it all in perspective for us, sincerely thanking us for their work without making us out to be heroes and reminding us that the next time we go to the beach for fun, we could continue this work. Heads cocked as she said, "I always have gloves in my backpack. You never know what you could find."

I faked a nod. It seemed like good advice to give teenagers, even if I was not going to take it myself, and I certainly was not going to take it. It seemed like an eccentric hippie thing to do. But a few weeks later I was at another beach where I found myself picking up trash, gloveless, and wishing I had gloves in my bag. Kimberly had changed the way I saw the landscape. Now every little piece of trash reminds me of her heartfelt commitment. And I know in my body what it feels like to spend a few minutes picking up trash, like a swimmer who knows without thinking what the backstroke feels like. Now I can fall into it like a familiar routine.

I still don't carry gloves. But I do pick up trash like Kimberly does, especially when I find it on a beach or near a storm drain. And I carry hand sanitizer, for the next bottle of piss.

The next evening, Kimberly arrived bearing huge bags of fabric, which she dumped out on the tables after dinner. That evening would be devoted to artistic reflection. With her, we would cut and design fabric to make quilted banners for our home church, bringing the Blue Theology program visibly back to Montclair Presbyterian Church. She had built quite a collection of ocean-themed cotton prints, and she was infectiously enthusiastic about them. After we had spent a while poring over the colors and patterns, she gave us guidance on cutting fabric out in the shape of sunfish, sea stars, turtles, and albatross, and we pinned our designs in place with about a million pins. Later Kimberly would take the pinned pieces home with her and spend several evenings running them through her embroidery machine until everything was held together. She mailed the banners to us that winter, and we designed a water-focused Lenten worship experience featuring the banners, although as it turned out, we had just one week to appreciate the banners in person before our plans were cut short by the arrival of Covid-19.

The quilt was the right metaphor, though, for our Blue Theology learning experience. A quilt is something you can make from scraps that might not look useful but that come together to make something new, leaving nothing to waste.

Blue Theology did a great job of quilting our lives together for the service of the ocean: some learning experiences here, some meditations there, some art and science and song— all stitched together lovingly to create a piece of art that will call our hearts to service whenever we see it. Our quilted banners were group projects, with pieces of each of our ideas woven in. Fred was obsessed with making an accurate albatross, Melvie got deep into her quest to represent sand crabs, and Mimi was careful to group the sea creatures in the appropriate ecological zone. Grace was not feeling artistic that night, but she set herself at the ironing station and stayed busy ironing any little scrap of fabric anyone brought her. Jim, though decidedly not an artist, cheerfully did whatever task anyone told him to do and cracked jokes left and right. Everyone had their place.

In the end, all our fingerprints were on the banners, and Kimberly's creative energy pulled it all together. None of us would have been able to do this project alone, but Kimberly was the kind of leader who made it possible. She donated her scrap fabric collection, her time, and the use of her embroidery machine, and then stepped back to let us create our own sense of meaning. She did not boss us around or tell us what to do, but she did give us a prompt and expect us to articulate an answer: What did today's work and learning mean to you? This kind of guidance is as important as the goal-setting kind. Once we have had an experience, we need to reflect on what it meant to us. We need to be able to narrate where we have been.

We always have a report-back session in church a few days or weeks after a mission trip. We take over the sermon section of the service and put up a slideshow with our photo memories. We hand the microphone around the youth group, asking each to focus on what was most important. For some, this is their first big public speaking experience and causes a bit of nerves. Others—mainly the theater crowd—get up with great confidence. I ask them all to write their thoughts ahead of time. Gathering ideas is an important part of the reflection process. And a two-minute time limit is far tighter than most of us realize. We need to pull those ideas in like a net of fish. What was the *most* important thing?

Someone providing care for this second spiritual need does not take over the conversation to provide their own interpretation. They do not tell us what to say or believe or do. Rather they prompt us, as Kimberly did, to wonder what was the most meaningful part of our day. When they hear us name something important, they lift it up again, affirming it, clarifying it. Like the swim coach who watched us improvise a rescue and then sat us down to tell us what he saw, a good leader watches closely and reflects back to the group what seemed important. Like Kimberly later laboring with her embroidery machine, they take our scattered thoughts and ideas and tack them down solidly in place. Yes, they say—this is what you did. This is what you said. This is what you said it means. They resist the urge to improve our work but use their skill to strengthen and affirm it. They help us name the most important thing out of the net of our gathered experiences, and they amplify it for us.

Providing ecologically informed spiritual care for people to address this second spiritual need is now, for me, a matter of asking the question WWKD (What would Kimberly do?). It's not about shaming or "should-ing." We can help others by sharing our commitment and helping people come alongside us. Reminding them they could keep gloves in their backpack. Staying focused, staying strong. And over and over again affirming what we see in them, saying yes to their learnings, their commitments, their newfound stamina.

Mulching Muscle Memory

> Being in youth group and being taught "you need
> to go out and do this" makes a huge difference. It
> becomes second nature. This is your duty to do: go
> out there and mulch for hours and get something
> done.
>
> —MELVIE, eighteen

It was the fall of 2019 and California was on fire, burning from
the rural Oregon border down to the expensive suburbs of
Los Angeles. A record-breaking hot, dry, and windy October
led to a terrible fall fire season. Winds were so high that a
fire leaped across the Carquinez Strait, the narrowest part of
the San Francisco Bay but still a terrifying long jump of nearly
3,500 feet across water. We were blanketed in smoke, and the
skies turned an eerie peach-pink. We had hoped to avoid
such terrible fires that year, and Pacific Gas & Electric had
turned off several neighborhoods' power to reduce risk. By
Halloween the lights had been turned off two or three times,

depending on where you lived. The wind brought trees down with terrible randomness. Walking the darkened streets of our little "village" center in the hills was creepy. Most businesses were closed, though some stayed open in the dark, trying valiantly to make ends meet with cash sales and handwritten receipts. Some supermarkets had a generator truck; smaller places made do with lanterns or just closed shop. Lots of hourly workers went without work, without pay. The coffee shop to which I am loyal made me a cold brew and offered a few pastries for sale before they ran out of ice and gave up for a few days. We could not charge electronic devices or get cell phone service, much less Wi-Fi. Around me people were jumpy, nervous, irritable, and angry at PG&E, which could have, should have, ought to have (we said, with perfect hindsight) modernized its equipment more and avoided the fire risk.

The youth of our church were due to go on retreat to Camp Cazadero. We had a thirty-year-long tradition of going up to the camp, nestled above the Russian River in a beautiful, superrustic, no-cell-reception kind of place. But fire season threatened the trip to Caz. Roads were closed on the way there, and a fire burned not far from the camp. The youth crossed their fingers and toes and we all prayed. They wanted, of course, to go to A&W for a root beer (it's tradition!) and to sleep in bunks in the possibly haunted lodge and to muck around in the foggy woods playing capture the flag.

On Sunday morning our congregation met for worship without electricity. People scooted up to the front pews to hear me preach without a microphone, and I went a little hoarse. That night the youth group gathered in the dark. We meet at

7 p.m., so the light had already drained out of the sky when we arrived. Driving through the dark neighborhood, with no lights except occasional lanterns in the neighbors' windows, was surreal. I got to church before the students and put electric candles out on the stairs and in the hallways. I found glow sticks in a cupboard and threw one to each person as they entered—Heads up! Catch! As we circled up for conversation, they insisted on raising a glow stick to indicate they wanted to talk. I excused them from any reading, given the small print and our lighting constraints, and told them a Bible story instead. But the conversation kept veering back to an anxious topic:

"So can we go to Caz?"

"Maybe!" I would say, firmly. "Maybe not."

"Are they on fire?"

"I don't think so. But their region was completely evacuated today, and it looks like their power has been off for two days. The Kincaid fire is not too far away, and there are at least two more days of extreme windstorms coming this week."

"If we can't go, can we have an overnight here in the church instead?"

"Maybe. We'll see."

"I hope we go to Caz," Nazareth said mournfully. "You don't know how much I am sacrificing to get there."

"I'm missing *three rehearsals*," Melvie sighed loudly. "And I barely even know how to operate the spotlight. Which is literally my job . . . ha!" We laughed with her.

"Well, I'm missing a soccer game!" William said. I do not remember William ever missing a soccer game. He wants to go pro.

Nazareth rows crew and was unwilling to be topped in this contest of who was sacrificing the most. "I'm missing a *regatta*, y'all. It's a *big* deal. But my team is going to have to manage without me. Because I have my priorities in place, and I am *tired* of missing church retreats for crew."

"That's right, you haven't been on retreat with us for like . . . a year?"

"A year and a half. I know. It's inexcusable. But I'm going with you this year, and I don't care what they say." People leaned over and gave her fist bumps and glow stick bumps, saluting her priorities.

"Here's to Caz! May it be safe and not on fire!" We raised our glow sticks and cheered.

The Kincaid fire continued to burn that week. At times it was terrifying. Fortunately, it claimed no human lives, perhaps because Californians were collectively getting the hang of the pack-up-get-out routine, but the loss of buildings and animal and plant life was still sobering. Each morning I would get up and check the news, praying and crossing my fingers. The winds died down after a few days and the power came back on here, even while people were still evacuated up in Sonoma and fire crews were still out fighting. Smoke came and went with the winds, but the air stayed dry and hot. I watched the weather and kept praying.

The day before we were due to go to Caz, CalFire announced the Kincaid fire was finally fully contained. The roads reopened, the power went back on again, and we breathed easy.

Who am I kidding? We did not breathe easy. Yes, we sighed with relief, but we were exhausted from the effort of watching, listening, worrying. We headed to Camp Caz tense with weeks of built-up nerves. We arrived and filled the lodge with buzzing anxious energy.

The youth know the retreat rules, including this one: you are allowed to stay up as late as you want, as long as adult chaperones are up too. This translates into "you can stay up as long as Talitha's having fun." Once I get bored, I get sleepy, and that is the end of that. So they ply me with hot chocolate and ask deep questions and perform improv games. They work hard to earn their late-night privileges. But this year none of us could sleep, and with the tension of fire season all around us, we did not need hot chocolate to stay up. They got late nights without even working for them.

I had spent so much time working on contingency plans in case Caz was evacuated or powered down or just too smoky to be healthy that I had not spent much time making the actual retreat programming—the plans for how the retreat would go hour by hour and what arts and crafts supplies we would need. I had barely been able to talk to the camp staff between power outages. So I had packed a random assortment of craft materials and asked God to inspire us. I trusted we would find something meaningful in our stay—like those underprepared Sundays when the sermon falls flat but the hymns pull you through.

The camp staff at Caz saved the day by having tons of activities for us to do. A huge tree had come down in a wind-storm, and they had cut it into chunks with chain saws and chippers, but work still remained that could be done only by people power. We could stack logs in a safe place to be used as firewood in the rainy season. Spreading the chips around as mulch would protect the other trees, lock in moisture, and reduce fire danger. We linked this work into our theme—loving the world that God so loves—and committed ourselves to two hours of labor on Saturday morning.

We had, however, stayed up far too late on Friday night. We cleaned up from Saturday breakfast and trooped outside with a bit of bleariness in our eyes. The camp staff in their ranger hats and cheerful smiles tried to pep us up.

"Mulching is really important fire-prevention work! It could make the difference between safety and a big fire."

"I know you all really care about God's creation. Well, here's a chance to show it!"

I wish I could say we did a good job faking some enthusiasm, but our baseline exhaustion was obvious. We mustered up, though. I put on my best camp-counselor face and got Fred, William, and Naz interested in rolling and stacking the heavy logs. They were, after all, missing some athletic practice this weekend, and a little dare went a long way to motivate them. Anna and Adrian, a young chaperoning couple, found some music to play for the rest of the crew who were shoveling mulch. They had brought their young daughter Cora with them, and she was perhaps the only well-rested person on the retreat, as she had napped in the car on the way up. So Cora set the pace. Sheepishly, as if embarrassed to let a six-year-old outwork them, the group slowly rumbled to life. We picked up our buckets and rakes and shovels.

Mulching is boring. Stacking logs involves a little strategy and skill, but mulching is just sheer grunt work. An enormous pile had been dropped there by the chipper, and our task was to spread it around the trees. We set to work: filling a bucket, carrying it away, dumping it, and raking it even.

Half an hour in, we were thoroughly bored. We experimented with techniques, wondering if we could throw the mulch out of the buckets evenly enough to not need raking. We switched tools, seeing whether each person liked the shovel or the pitchfork more. Like swimmers switching strokes to keep from getting overtired, we rotated, trying out different things in turn.

An hour in and the mood was getting a little silly, perhaps due to the candy we ate to keep our energy levels up. Our snack break could have lasted a half hour if Cora had not been so enthusiastic to get back to work. We rustled up what energy we could find and groaned our way into working again. New techniques continued to proliferate as we switched around to keep from getting too bored or sore. I saw two people pair up over a bucket, with one shoveling and the other carrying and dumping: multitasking, two tasks at once! (I looked again and saw it was actually three tasks: flirting at the same time. Noted.)

Ninety minutes in and, between yawns, I saw a curious foot shuffle emerge. If you shuffled down from the top of the mulch pile, you could kick a bucketful of mulch into your bucket, especially if you had another friend standing there with a foot braced on the bucket to keep it in place. Minimizing labor while still keeping momentum—these are the things you learn when you are on your last ounces of energy and patience.

The end was in sight—not that the nearly endless task was done but that Debbie came out and let us know she would need lunch helpers in the kitchen soon. We could use this motivation to finish strong. Adrian DJ'd us quite effectively, each song getting a little faster and more fun. The next time my sore back needed a break, I scooted around taking pictures of each of our workers, cheerleading about the homestretch as I went.

"I bet you can't finish that pile before lunch!" one of the camp staff dared us, and reluctantly we looked around and decided to accept their challenge. Anna, Adrian, and I chirped encouragement at an increasingly frenzied pace as the end drew near. Even with our cheering and the energizing soundtrack, though, the group barely limped across the finish line with a fizzle and a sigh.

But we were proud of ourselves. Nobody was quite at their best, except perhaps Cora, who was tireless 'til the end. Some spent a little more time giggling than others, but we all kept going. We could all know in our bodies what the love language of "acts of service" could feel like when spoken lovingly to God's creation. It feels like tired arms, shuffling feet, mulch mysteriously found in your ponytail, and perhaps a little blister from the shovel handle. Nobody was under any illusion that this work could save this beloved camp from the fire danger it was so often in. But it stuck with us. Like the beach cleanup habit that I adopted weeks after meeting Kimberly in Monterey, mulching was lodged in our muscle memories.

We were all tired and no one really wanted to do it, we just wanted to play and be kind of crazy, but we all did it anyways. And we were playing music and stuff. . . . It was nice to be like "we're going to do this," a collective understanding that we were going to do it together. It felt good after, like a really good accomplishment.

—Olivia, sixteen

Part Four
RIDING THE SWELLS

God saw how corrupt the earth had become, for all
the people on earth had corrupted their ways. So
God said to Noah, "I am going to put an end to all
people, for the earth is filled with violence because
of them."

—GENESIS 6:12–13 NIV

The third spiritual need is interpersonal accountability. Here
we get into conflicts, hurt one another, clean up our messes,
and learn to take responsibility for how our words and actions
affect those around us. Here we deal with dramatic swells and
floods of powerful emotions: righteous anger, deep betrayal,
heavy sadness, and everything in between. Here we learn to
ride those intense waves, to stay afloat, and not to kick our
fellow swimmers in the head.

Camp Glenkirk, where I worked as a camp counselor, regularly took campers canoeing down the Shenandoah River.
We drilled them ahead of time with a canoe in the camp pool,

tipping and bailing and reorienting, shouting clear com-
mands to keep them from losing control of their canoe. We
taught and practiced visual signs too—learning paddle positions that could communicate important information when
we drifted out of shouting range. Then we would pack up the
canoes on a trailer and make our way to what we all reverently
called The River. We would put in upriver in the morning,
with sandwich-and-granola lunches packed in dry bags, and
make our way fourteen miles downstream. We would teach
our campers how to navigate through the rapids, choosing
the deepest and fastest-moving sections rather than getting
stuck on the shallow rocky sections. Many first-time canoers
instinctively want to stay in shallower, slower water, so we
coaxed them past their caution. In fact, the shallow water is
not always the safest, as you are more prone to run aground
on rocks there. Deeper water, though it may look scary, is
actually a safer bet because the rocks are farther away, underneath you. And though slow and steady seems comfortable,
sometimes you need to steer toward the places where fast-
moving water will send your canoe shooting forward between
a chute of rocks. Turbulence is not always a sign of danger;
sometimes it is the only way forward.

My first year as counselor was a year of drought. Over and
over we ran aground in too-shallow sections and had to pick
up our canoes to carry them over the rocks. We invented word
games and songs to keep ourselves entertained. The drought-
year trip took about ten hours. The next year we had terrible thunderstorms and superhigh water levels, so we left the
canoes at camp and rented rafts instead. We put the whole

crew in helmets and shot down the same route in an exhilarating three hours; you can go a lot faster when the water runs deep, and though wearing helmets feels scary, they are essential when you are inadvertently turning underwater somersaults.

To meet our third spiritual need, we need to overcome our caution and steer for the deeper, faster water. We need to be able to communicate clearly and work together. When the intensity level is low, we need to look for depth and turbulence to show us the way through. When the water is deep, we need to hold on, paddle hard, and communicate like hell.

Sam interrupted me at an online youth group meeting in 2020 while we all sheltered in place during a serious summer surge of Covid-19. I had just begun the meeting with some solemn words about the difficult times we were living through.

"Sorry, Talitha, but can I say something?" she asked, and of course I gave her the go-ahead. She took a deep breath and launched in.

"I just get a little mad when people say 'these difficult times.' That's like the biggest understatement you've ever heard. Are you really seeing what's happening? Like, come on, people, call it like it is: these are terrible times. Hospitals are full and people are dying, and we don't even know what to do for this disease or whether we can make a vaccine or when we'll ever get out of it. And online education is basically useless, and people are unemployed and desperate."

She paused, just barely, for breath.

"And Black people are getting murdered by police, and the cops are getting away with it. And nobody is doing anything about climate change. And so even if we get through the pandemic and then, like, everyone is so excited to, you know, 'get back to normal,' but normal was kind of awful too. And things are just extra terrible now. So, I mean, just don't say these are difficult times. They are way beyond difficult. They are terrible, terrible times."

I was chastened and struck the phrase "difficult times" from my pandemic vocabulary. I could see, when Sam pointed it out to me, how much the phrase revealed the privilege that was insulating me from raw suffering; I was distraught but safe in my home while others wept in hospital parking lots and had panic attacks at their essential jobs. Trust a teenager to look at the world and see the angst. Speak of the world without that angst, and they know you are not seeing the world as they see it; you are not in the deep water with them.

Sam was my prophet that day. She spoke truth as clear as a bell. It was an honor to receive that correction from her, and from then on I could never hear someone say "difficult times" without thinking of her.

Sam has a natural boldness that makes her good at helping people through the interpersonal exchanges of the third spiritual need. Another teenager might have just rolled their eyes at the overused phrase "difficult times" and not said anything, letting the annoyance fester into resentment, feeling stuck and hopeless. But Sam had the confidence, the clarity, and the communication skills to stop me and offer her perspective. She knew speaking up would make a difference, and she knew she wanted to have her pastor on the same page she was on. Speaking up takes guts, taking a stand for something important. She steered us off the rocks and toward the deep waters where despair and anger run fast and cold.

Chapter 14

Yelling at God

How do you deal with the existential angst of it all?
[I asked].

Bold of you to assume that we do.

—MIMI, eighteen

In the fall of 2018, California was on fire. The towns of Paradise and Malibu went up simultaneously like tinderboxes. Some residents escaped with only their lives, and some were less lucky. We were blanketed with smoke blowing south on a hot dry wind from Paradise. We strapped masks on our faces, bought new air filters, and stayed indoors.

We were scared. Your nose ought to be your early warning system for a fire near you, but now you have to rely on your eyes and ears and smoke detectors and cell phone alerts to keep you safe. And it was hot, dry, and windy: fire weather here in Oakland too.

My husband got the cat carriers out of the basement, just in case our neighborhood went up in flames and we had to evacuate. Fires were all we could think about, waking and sleeping. We debated whether driving or biking would be safer in the case of an evacuation. In a preemptive evacuation, we could drive no matter how slow; in a true emergency, bike paths could get us out faster, through or around traffic. Michael's brother was our evacuation destination, and he lived only three miles away in relative safety on the flatlands. Riding the brakes downhill the whole way, we could bike the distance easily. But could we balance the cat carriers on our bikes? We added rope and bungee cords to the emergency stash and ordered more respirator masks.

On November 9, when Paradise had been burning for three days, I was scheduled to take our youth group to Camp Cazadero for our annual fall retreat. The week before, at our Sunday night meeting, the question "Are you ready for Caz?" had prompted a chorus of excited conversation. Ray bellowed, "Capture the flag!" and pumped their fists in excitement. Melvie pulled photos up on her phone from last year: ferns, fog, and dewy spiderwebs around the wooded outdoor chapel. Two seventh graders would be coming on their first retreat, and they each had their questions about roommates and sleeping bags. Everyone giggled about the spooky true story we would tell the newbies about the origins of Camp Caz—it's tradition! And thirteen-year-old Dean reminded everyone to bring three dollars for root beer floats on the way home. We always stopped at the one A&W in the Bay Area on our way home, and the remembrance of that rare taste had become a nostalgic anchor for all these young and growing memories. Dean was just on his second retreat, but the A&W stop was essential for him—it's tradition! We were all looking forward to Caz.

But on Thursday, day two of the Paradise fire, we heard that Caz was directly under the huge and stinking plume of smoke that rose from Paradise and made its slowly expanding way out to sea. I thought about the risks of smoke inhalation and changed some plans for the weekend: no nature walks, chapel indoors. Capture the flag canceled for the sake of our lungs. Dean texted me, worrying about cancellation, and I tried to reassure him we could do other fun (indoor) things. And I watched the air quality index (AQI) like a hawk. The AQI is measured at various weather stations, and my app would show a color, a cartoon, and a number—from green smiling "go ahead" at 25, to yellow frowning "caution" at 100, to red and masked "danger" at 150+. Friday morning the AQI was yellow in Oakland, orange at Caz. I thought it looked okay . . . but on second thought, my lungs were burning after just a walk to the coffee shop on the corner here at home, and some of our youth had asthma. I checked again after lunch and found an alert level higher than I had ever seen before: the AQI at Caz had shot up to 350, dark purple, and the cartoon character was wearing an actual gas mask.

I walked next door and up the stairs to the church office and flopped in a swivel chair. We were supposed to leave on retreat in three hours.

"I don't think I can do this," I said.

Senior pastor Ben stood behind the chair next to mine, drumming his fingers on its back. His interest was more than professional; all three of his teenage children were packed and ready to go on the retreat with me.

"How bad is it up there?"

I showed him the app. He grimaced.

"We'd be better off staying home and having the retreat at church. But everyone's so miserable here already," I sighed.

"That we are," he said. "Our house is the biggest gripe fest I've seen. They all really want to get out. But I keep telling them—not in this air."

Willetta, a church volunteer who was sitting nearby, folding bulletins for Sunday, softly put in, "It's too bad this isn't the retreat where you take them to Tahoe."

Tahoe. What an idea. The drive is not that much farther, but it is uphill in the mountains, and upwind from the fire. I pulled it up on my app, and a smiling, unmasked green cartoon face beckoned. I thought we might lose the payment we had made for the cabins at Caz, but the church might think that price was worth paying for everyone's health. When I do not know what my gut instincts are, I trust Ben's. I looked to him. His pastoral calm was stricken through with parental anxiety.

"If I were you, Talitha, I would get out of here."

The decision was made. We scrapped all plans and reorganized our retreat. The people on the phone from the Presbyterian Conference Center sympathized as they booked our cabins. Willetta, Ben, and I all called the families of the youth to let them know of the change and to ask them to throw a warmer jacket in the car. I ran down the block to my house, nerves jangling, and finished packing my own bag. I knew I had forgotten at least one important thing in the rush (as it turned out, it was my prescription meds), but I felt sure that we had made the right decision.

In the parking lot we handed out N95 respirator masks to the tune of "OMG, can you believe we're going to Tahoe?" Parents hugged me, thanking me for finding a healthy solution. The youth peppered me with excited questions and exclaimed about how bad the air already was.

"My app says the smoke is going to get even worse when we come home," Melvie lamented, punching her sleeping bag into the back of a minivan.

"Can we stay an extra day? They might cancel school on Monday," Fred pitched hopefully, looking around at the circle of parents who didn't really think so.

"I can't wait to play outsiiiiiide," Ben's son William howled through his mask.

"There isn't an A&W in Tahoe, is there?" Dean asked me, wistfully. "We're going to have to skip it this year, aren't we?"

We took a group photo (it's tradition!) in the parking lot, with our respirator masks on. (You can see the ominous color of the sky in the photo, behind the trees.) We said a prayer and said goodbye to the parents with a little more emotion than usual. I wished I had been able to hug my husband goodbye, just in case, but he was off at work in San Francisco, so I texted him instead. And we piled into the minivans, and we were off.

Now we were headed toward clean air, but we had to drive through Mordor to get there: the red zone heading toward Sacramento, much closer to Paradise, where the thick smoky haze reduced visibility and traffic to a foggy crawl. Gazing into it, the air looked much like the cool fog we are familiar with in San Francisco, but it stank, and it turned every light red, from the dropping sun to the headlights of oncoming traffic. Melvie and Sam, in the middle seats of the minivan, had their phones held to the windows to take artsy photos of the awful air. Ray was riding shotgun next to me, and they had put their phone down next to them with a sigh. They gazed into the eerie haze, narrowed their eyes, and slumped even more deeply in their seat.

"This is okay," they said, gesturing vaguely at the red smoke.

Nobody knew what to say.

"It's okay, we just have to get used to it. No breathing for a few weeks every fall, just like last year. This is just going to be normal for us."

I grunted assent to Ray's assessment, my eyes on the road, as I reminded myself that the past two autumn seasons, featuring the Santa Rosa fire in 2017 and now Paradise burning in 2018, made up a good percentage of the autumns the teenagers could remember. They were all born in the early 2000s. Climate change was not slowing down, and the grown-ups in charge were not taking drastic action to stop it, so the young people did not have much reason to expect things to change for the better. To long-sighted adults like me, the fire still seemed like an anomaly: two fire seasons in a row, perhaps, but still just two irregular seasons among regular autumns marked by pumpkin spice, cozy sweater weather, and long-standing fall traditions. To the youth, this was not just one irregular season—it was their life. And these huge fires were now a central part of their landscape. Wearing respirator masks was as much a fall tradition as the cozy sweaters were. Even if fall *should* smell like apple pies, root beer, and the musty old lodge at camp Caz, to them it also indelibly smelled like smoke.

"Yeah, two years in a row is really becoming a pattern," I said.

"Whatever, we can deal with it. Breathing isn't the only thing in life," Ray said, shrugging their shoulders.

The others in the car laughed a bit and fell silent. We do not know how to deal with it. Our lungs hurt.

"I mean, what's God doing in all of this?" Ray asked. "Are they just throwing up their hands and going, 'Okay, humans, time for you to destroy the world, I guess. Have fun!'"

I realized, with something between a thrill and a chill, that we were moving into a Big Conversation—we were headed toward deep waters. Ray was ready to talk. They were ready to argue with God.

"It's okay. Whatever." Ray gestured at the sky, sinking into their hoodie.

"Huh, I wonder what God's thinking," I hazarded, hoping for more of Ray's theological imagination.

"Well, God was okay with letting us ruin the world with a climate apocalypse, so I feel like God *wasn't* really thinking."

From the back seat, young Dean piped up. "I don't think God's okay with it. God cares about the world and wants it to stay beautiful."

"Yeah, but God put us in charge, which was The. Stupid-est. Decision. Ever. God *really* messed up on this one." Ray's voice was icy and sure with all the authority of a high school junior silencing a middle schooler. You wouldn't dare break that silence, would you?

Nobody dared.

We stared at the feverish skies.

"Huh," I said, finally daring. "What do you think God should do?"

Ray narrowed their eyes and looked out the window.

"Make it rain and put out the fires," William sighed.

"Wouldn't that be nice," Melvie agreed.

"That's not reasonable to expect, though," Sam pushed back. "Like, is it normal for God to just break the laws of weather and nature? The news said we weren't expecting any rain for a week. I think that's magical thinking."

"Yeah, I think that would be magic," Ray said dismissively. "It would be nice, but we shouldn't count on it."

"I don't think God does magic tricks," I said, slowly, carefully, trying to formulate a theologically sound contribution. "Although if it rained right now, I would thank God anyway."

"What I think," Fred said, and I could see him in the rearview mirror smirking with a clever look, "is that if you can thank God for rain, you can also yell at God for no rain." Fred's natural irreverence takes him easily over what could be a barrier of piety; there really is no such barrier for him.

"Right on," I mimed a high-five for Fred, over my shoulder.

"You would yell at God?" Dean asked, looking at me, a little surprised that his pastor did not consider Fred's idea heretical.

"Why not? The Bible is full of prayers that are basically yelling," I said. "It's just that we don't read them quite as often."

"If the dude upstairs is asleep at the wheel, maybe more yelling prayers would wake him up," Fred offered, and he was gratified with the laughter he was going for.

In moments like these, I am so grateful that our church has a solid tolerance for impiety. It would be spiritually stifling if we always had to express ourselves toward God in a thankful manner, even when we feel unthankful. Our church members might in fact err a bit much on the other side, taking pride in the attitude of "look at us skirting heresy!" But they came by it honestly, a legacy of their 1960s "question everything" philosophy. They love it when I demonstrate in a children's sermon that we can pray with heads bowed, or holding hands, or with a fist raised to the sky. But the internalized "supposed to" of performative piety is still ingrained. So I keep reminding them how okay it is to be deeply and seriously angry with God.

"I'd rather have an honest prayer than a fake one," I said. "Just like with people, like if you're mad at me, please tell me. Don't be quiet and polite."

"Meh," Ray shrugged. "It doesn't matter much, though. What are you yelling *for*? We're still all gonna die."

"I'd rather go down yelling, probably," Fred said.

"It's probably better to yell than to repress your anger?" Sam posited thoughtfully.

"It's okay, though," Ray said, stretching and expertly cracking their neck. "I mean everyone dies sometime."

"Of course. Nobody escapes it, not even Jesus," I affirmed, checking the rearview mirror to assess our timider back-seat participants. They looked okay—they were staring out the window, but their faces didn't look like despair. Perhaps they had heard this perspective before. In 2018, I hadn't. At least, not in these stark terms.

"Everyone's gonna die," Ray continued, "and it's nice to hope that your life will be purposeful, but you know what, not everyone gets that. Like I would wish I were known for saving the world, but maybe my purpose is to be one of the billions of people who just die early because of climate change. I can be okay with that."

Ouch, that was not quite what I meant to affirm a moment ago. I let out a pained sound, sucking air through my teeth.

"And maybe the small group of people who are left on earth after it's ruined will learn from our mistakes and I'm just one of the mistakes they learn from. Or maybe they don't learn, but, hey, we did what we had to do."

Sam jumped in from the middle seat. "Yeah, that's how I feel too. Like the earth will survive, it's a living organism, and we're the infection on it, and the earth is cooking up a fever to kill us off. Like, I hope I leave some good art behind and have a good time in my life, and I'll do what I can to slow climate change down and make the world a little better, but I don't see us or even God turning this situation around. And the people who survive it are going to be the rich people who survive at the expense of the rest of us, so they aren't going to learn from us little people."

Melvie was not feeling this nihilism. "Y'all are bringing me down with your attitude. You don't need to be so cynical. Look, this is the time for a wake-up call. People see how bad it's going to be, and they take action and stop it."

"I can imagine that happening," I offered. "That could be the answer to our prayers: people paying attention. This could be the big moment . . . like Moses leading the Hebrew people out of slavery."

"Nah, we're so far gone already," Ray blew back.

"What would it take for us to turn the world around?" I ventured, trying to open the conversation up to more hopeful avenues. Because I still believe *with God all things are possible*. I do believe that, and even if I cannot imagine the precise shape of it, I have a vague hope for a worldwide moral awakening, a realization that all nations and peoples must tackle this together.

But if I started preaching my hope right then, flexing my pastoral authority, the openness and realness of this conversation would be over. So I threw out some leading questions instead. "What could possibly save us? What do you think?"

"We just all need to do what we can to help, and not get discouraged," said Dean, doggedly hopeful, or perhaps just too young still to have stared down the abyss like the high schoolers were doing.

"It would take a restructuring of all the money and power systems in the world, which isn't gonna happen," Sam said quickly and confidently.

"Yup, no way it gets fixed under capitalism," Fred said, "and I don't think capitalism is going away."

"It would take a really loud wake-up call, which *is* happening right now!" exclaimed Melvie, gesturing with both hands at the red sky out the window.

Ray shook their head darkly.

"It would take a real miracle."

We rode in silence for a while and slowly broke up the intensity of that conversation with lighter subjects: looking forward to our dinner stop, a silly selfie texted over from the youth riding in another van.

"Is that an A&W?!" William suddenly pointed and asked. All heads turned—I turned mine back promptly, remembering I was the driver—but alas, it was some random store whose logo started with a big A.

"I was hoping we could keep the tradition and still get root beers," William said, deflated.

"I hope we can go to Caz next year," Dean said wistfully. "Do you think there will be another fire then?"

"Probably not," I said encouragingly (oh, how little I knew).

"Probably," Ray, Sam, and Melvie said at exactly the same time.

Chapter 15
Forgiving and Unburdening

I've been feeling bad about it ever since.

—REBECCA, fifteen

Our third spiritual need expresses itself in how we relate to other people. We need to be able to work through conflict, to take responsibility for our actions, to forgive and confess and make amends. We need to be able to safely ride the swift swells of emotion that show up when we disagree with others or when others have hurt us. We need to go ahead and yell at God. We need to bring ourselves back up to the surface again when we have been tumbled around by powerful waves of anger, resentment, guilt, or shame. We need to communicate clearly with those around us: the fellow swimmer who has just kicked us in the head, the pastor who has spoken as if this apocalypse is not really a big deal, and the grandparent who has just told us they do not believe in climate change. We need to steer away from the shallowness of polite disagreement and toward the rapids of accountability, even confrontation.

Someone whose need for interpersonal accountability is well met can handle disagreements without getting into blowup fights. They can admit when they are wrong. They have people they can trust to reflect the truth back to them, whether it is as simple as "You seem tired, dear," or as complex as "You just said something that made me feel hurt." They can give the same clarity in return, telling Grandma, "When you dismiss climate change, it hurts, because it feels like you're discounting my future." And they are secure in their relationship with God. They do not mind praying with a fist raised toward the sky; they know that God can handle their anger. If they have done something wrong, they do not need to punish themselves or wallow in guilt; they can confess and expect forgiveness.

Someone whose need for interpersonal accountability is not well met, who is in deep need, may express it in two primary ways. In one direction—outward—they may be angry, prone to high-drama situations, always getting into arguments, always ready to kick back when kicked. In the other direction—inward—they may be resentful, disconnected, and poised for disappointment. They may isolate themselves out of a sullen sureness that people will hurt them. But whichever direction they go, they will have a hard time taking responsibility for the situation they find themselves in; it will always be Someone Else's fault. The healing direction will be for them to find what they *do* have agency over and focus on that instead of blaming others.

When this need is deep and unmet, we always carry some angsty energy toward Someone Else. Often that is a person, but it might also be God, whom we expect to behave a certain way. If only God would rescue us, we wail like the proverbial flood victims on the roof, while letting a lifeboat pass right by, rowed by angels in disguise. What we expect is an ecological rescue that requires nothing of us, a deus ex machina who will scoop us up straight to safety. This image of God is a simplistic one that requires nothing on the part of humanity, while God waves a magic wand and makes the carbon in the atmosphere disappear. Many people have uncritically accepted a view of God as the purveyor of a magical power—that guy in the sky—and think that to believe otherwise would be impious. To get unstuck from this magical view, we must redefine our relationship with God. Just as we negotiate new relationships with our parents as we grow up, we move into a more mature relationship with God, one that acknowledges each party has responsibility.

Where this spiritual need is well met, we are clear about what does and does not belong to us. We know each swimmer is responsible for keeping an eye on the kicking legs of the person in front of them. We can confess when we have done wrong, and we can help others talk about their wrongdoing as well. We know each human is responsible for their actions and inactions, and we know that God is not a puppet master forcing people to do the right thing. We can pray for rescue, but we know God will ask us to use our own arms to climb into the lifeboat.

In seminary, egged on by enthusiastic blog readers, I decided to take up the social experiment of wearing clerical collars in public. It is a worthy experiment for any person who plans to wear the collar for official (pastoral) business to also take some time wearing it around town—to see what expectations the general public has of ministers. I have rarely worn one on a plane, for the fear of being buttonholed for hours by a seatmate who needs to explain all their issues with religion. But I have worn one on a cross-country train trip. I put my collar on and rode an Amtrak from Oregon to New York. It was 2009, so I tweeted about the experience by texting from my flip phone. Friends retweeted me, and I would not say I went viral, but I was famous in my small world—at least to the point that a social-media-savvy Presbyterian stopped me in a train station asking if I was Madam Future Moderator (my Twitter handle at the time). My conversations were real tweetable gold though. From a truck driver as he boarded the train: "I'll have to watch my language around you, ma'am. That collar scared the hell out of me," followed soon by, "Oh, shit. Sorry, ma'am. I mean, sorry, Rev. I mean . . . ah, shit." He and I actually formed a rather comfortable friendship over the next two days or so until we arrived in Chicago and transferred to different trains.

Boarding my New York–bound train in Chicago, I saw a mother dropping off her teenage daughter. The girl might have been fifteen, and she was to be traveling alone. Her nerves jangled like the buzz of an ungrounded electric circuit.

Mom went around the waiting room talking to every Amtrak employee she could corner, without satisfaction and with increasing frustration, until she finally spotted two young men in uniform—seamen recruits, I think—and placed her daughter firmly and confidently in their care. The girl proceeded to talk their ears off, chattering nonstop as we made our way to the platform and boarded the train.

A few stops later, as afternoon lengthened into evening, I was sitting and reading in a booth in a café car. I saw all three of them enter together, the girl still talking. Her handlers, evidently a bit fatigued, encouraged her to sit down by me while they went to get a beverage. Down she flopped and cheerfully introduced herself.

"Hi! I'm Rebecca!"

"I'm Talitha. Hello."

And here comes the question about the clerical collar, in three . . . two . . . one . . .

"So are you a priestess or something?"

The corners of my mouth twitched up involuntarily as visions of pagan rites danced in my head.

"Kind of. I'm studying to be a pastor."

"That's Christian, right?"

"Yes, Presbyterian."

She nodded sagely as if this put me entirely in my place.

"So can you hear confessions yet, or do you have to wait until you're a real priestess?"

"Uh, that's actually an interesting question. In the Presbyterian Church, we do confession differently. We don't have, like, a booth and a priest sitting inside it."

"Oh. What do you do?"

"Well, we all say a prayer of confession together in church and then have silence to pray. We don't believe you need a priest to go between the people and God."

"Oh. That's *really* nice."

"Are you Catholic, then?"

"Yeah. Well, kinda. My grandparents are super Catholic and they would go to confession four times a week if they could. They are always telling us to go with them to church, but we don't usually."

The recruits returned and sat in a booth just across the aisle from us. I was startled to see they had come back from the bar with sodas—ah, yes, they were probably all of nineteen years old. Old enough to fight, kill, or die for their country, and responsible enough to chaperone a nervous girl on the train, but not old enough to order a brew. I leaned across the aisle and shared my chocolate bar with the young men. Rebecca was still talking.

"My cousins in Michigan, I don't know if they're religious or not, I guess I'll find out when I get there. I haven't seen them since the wedding, and that was a while ago."

I nodded vaguely as she went on. This litany of identifying all one's religious and nonreligious family members is a usual part of the warm-up when people start talking to a person in a collar, but usually it just covers immediate family members, not all the way to cousins.

The young men at the table across handed the chocolate back and sent some beef jerky with it. Rebecca took a piece eagerly and watched me pass it on without taking any.

"Are you not hungry?"

"I'm okay. I'm a vegetarian," I said, feeling a bit apologetic about turning down the gift of table fellowship.

She nodded. "Why did you decide that?"

"Well, I've always avoided eating *too* much meat, because it's better for your health and better for the environment. But more recently my friends were slaughtering a chicken they had raised. So I was there, I watched, but I realized I couldn't kill the bird myself. It just isn't in me to kill something alive. So I stopped eating meat altogether."

"But it's okay if I eat it?"

I waved my hand. "Go on, don't worry!"

She stashed a bite in her cheek and chewed as she talked.

"My grandparents raised chickens and ate them until they had to move off the farm. They always used to tease us that they would make us kill them if we wanted chicken for dinner." She shuddered. "If I was really hungry like in the wilderness or something, I know I could do it because I've watched, but I'm glad I never had to. I never killed something, I mean, nothing bigger than a bug." She chewed thoughtfully. A moment later her hand flew to her mouth and her eyes bugged out wide.

"Wait, that's not true."

"What?" I asked, intrigued.

"I did kill something. Or I probably killed it. Oh, this is really bad. But I should tell you. It's like a confession."

"What happened?" I was really curious now—probably killed?

"I went to camp in the summer when I was younger. We had archery class every day. So I was shooting"—she fixed her body in an inexpert approximation of an archer's stance—"and it was far away, like . . . as far as those trees," she said, pointing out the window. "Anyway, I shot and I missed the target entirely."

She stopped and took a deep breath.

"And then we saw a rustling in the woods and heard a squeak. So we went to see, and there was this raccoon bleeding a little and looking zonked. So I had hit it, but the arrow kind of went off and just bumped it and didn't kill it, but it was hurt. We didn't want to touch it; it was kind of hissing at us, but we brought it a bowl of water and an old blanket in case it was in shock or something and needed to rest for a bit."

"It sounds like you did your best," I said. "You just missed the target. That was a really freaky accident, and I don't know what else you could have done."

"Well, it wasn't there in the morning, and so I thought it was okay. But later I heard the counselors talking about it when they thought I wasn't listening . . . and I think maybe they had actually taken it and buried it in the woods."

"Wow," I said. "How long ago was this?"

"Two years," she said. "And I've been feeling bad about it ever since."

I repeated my reassurances. "It wasn't your fault. Sometimes these things just happen. And you did everything you could afterward. It's okay to be sad about it, but I don't think you need to feel guilty."

"Thanks," she said, heaving a whole-body sigh. "That means a lot to me, considering you're practically a priestess."

Presbyterians have a complicated relationship with the priest-hood. We do ordain people to ministry, but not to the priesthood. We believe in the "priesthood of all believers," which means that the priestly duties—confession, absolution, intercession between people and God—are accessible to all. But that also means they are assigned to all, as a responsibility. None of us, pastor or not, can tell a person in need of confession that they should go somewhere else for that. By eliminating the intermediary power positions that gave certain people the authority to assign penance and decide for us what the appropriate amends might be, we have made absolution everyone's job.

I recognize the appeal of having a system where specialists are given the specific role of hearing confessions and offering assurance of forgiveness. I borrowed that role from this girl's Catholic faith when she turned to me trusting that I could hear her deep and distressing story. Like finding the recruits who can chaperone you on the train, you just need to find someone in clerical uniform and know their job is to hear you out, count the cost of your harm, and give you a carefully measured amount of forgiveness on behalf of God.

But those of us in less priestly religions have to do this for one another. Hearing a confession is one way of providing spiritual care. And providing assurance of pardon can be just as easy as it was in that booth on the train: "That's sad, but it sounds like you did your best. . . . I don't think you need to feel guilty." If you believe in a gracious God and can share that loving graciousness with someone in distress, no matter who you are, you can bring them relief.

Sometimes we go around the world consciously in need of confession, dragging around a guilty story like Rebecca's possibly dead raccoon. The pressure builds up, and we look for an outlet, which we might find in a church service, in an intimate conversation, or in private prayer. Once we blurt out the truth, we feel better. Then people can help us further to see what our responsibility is, and if need be, take action to remediate or make amends.

The word *sin* means "to miss the mark." It has its origin in an archery term, a measurement of how far off the target one strayed . . . whether or not a raccoon was hit. I told Rebecca this fact, which gave her "the good kind" of goose bumps, and she magnanimously told me in return that she would donate her archery story for my use in a sermon someday.

Sin is a fact of life. We all miss the mark, sometimes more spectacularly than other times, but nobody hits the bull's-eye straight on every time. And for Christians, Jesus raises the stakes to say that it is not enough to be mostly good or well controlled in our actions. Even our thoughts and feelings can be a kind of sin. "Be perfect," Jesus says, "as your heavenly Father is perfect" (Mark 5:48), and we all know we will miss that mark. Ecologically speaking, the bull's-eye we aim for—a life that helps and does not harm the earth—is terribly high and hard to hit. None of us can get it every time.

In the second spiritual need, we worked on course correction as we searched for our "marks," our guiding principles. The third spiritual need deals with the waves of emotion that happen when we miss those marks. It leads us into the process of confessing and making amends and navigating the interpersonal conflicts that happen when different people have different values. These bring up big feelings: guilt, shame, embarrassment, anger, defensiveness, resentment, even rage. So dealing with the third spiritual need is about learning to ride those waves of emotion with as much grace as possible. And providing spiritual care to someone in this need is about providing them a chance for unburdening, receiving forgiveness, taking responsibility, and making amends . . . even if you are not technically a priestess.

I worked as a cashier in the hippiest grocery store you have ever encountered: The Good Earth, Fairfax, California, established 1969. I had an actual fruitarian colleague who ate only food that the plant would give you of its own free will, such as fruit and nuts that fall off the tree (because if you pull a carrot from the ground, you kill it). Next to his principles, vegans were weaklings. He worked in the produce department, where he took loving care of the avocados and peaches. I never asked how he felt about stacking up all those carrot corpses for sale.

Cashiering in such an environmentally conscious place gave me lots of practice handling others' guilt, and not just about what they ate. Over and over the customers would arrive at my checkout line feeling overwhelmed with shame because they had forgotten their reusable bags in the car. So from my checkout lane, I practiced dispensing forgiveness. The customers would unload their groceries, stewing in guilt. By the time their purchases got down the conveyer belt to me, they could not hold it in anymore. The apologies spilled out, not to me, but to the store, their family, the city, the environment, to Al Gore, to the whole world. "I can't believe I forgot my canvas bags," they would wail. "I have a dozen in the back seat."

"It's okay!" I would chirp for the tenth time that day as I opened a paper bag for them. "I really care about the environment too, but it's hard to remember things like this!" They would apologize another time or two, sputtering, but I would cheerfully keep up my absolution, and eventually they would yield like a dam giving way under too much water pressure. Forgiveness would flow, and they would smile again.

Having practiced giving forgiveness so many times a day, you would think I could forgive my own self, wouldn't you? When I need a ten-cent paper bag? When I order an iced coffee without bringing a reusable straw? You would think that I would be able to look at myself in the mirror and say the same line I used in the checkout line: "It's okay, friend, you really care about the environment, but it's hard to remember things like this!" No, the guilt still tends to build up like floodwaters until someone else offers to release it for me. Forgiving ourselves in the mirror is good practice, but it does not compare to the power of hearing a trusted person (whether priestess or peer) say that they forgive you, and they think God does too. We need one another. Whether someone finds us on a train or in the grocery store, we can all be channels of God's grace.

Chapter 16

Are You with Me?

It was just nice to know that someone else felt angry as well.

—OLIVIA, fifteen, after a climate march

The third spiritual need is not just about repairing broken trust but also about maintaining relationships in various ways. We long to be surrounded and supported by healthy relationships, whether they are with other people, with God, or with the raccoons and creatures of the world, and so we learn how to live with others. Our everyday interactions do a lot to keep our relationships strong. We reach out to one another, we help with something, we send a birthday card or tag someone in an Instagram post. Apologies and forgiveness are important to keep our relationships maintained. But relationships are also maintained in invisible ways. If someone feels the same way we feel, our relationship is stronger, and likewise, it is weaker when they feel differently.

This subtle empathetic alignment keeps us connected even when we do not interact. We feel connected to other fans of our team when our team wins. We rejoice together when our candidate gets elected, and we give the side-eye to someone who sits back apathetically. Perhaps we feel connected to others in our class when we are all stressing together. If one high achiever in the class does not stress about the final exam, that person might be cut out of the communal stress connection. I was that kid in middle school. I handed my exams in early and sat at my desk looking bored while others shot desperate looks of exasperation my way. It did not help my social status. In high school, the tables were turned, and I was in the middle of the class, but having empathy for the teachers' pets did not stop me from feeling a terrible scorn when I watched them breeze through a difficult test while I still labored on. My reaction was quick and subconscious, nearly involuntary. We really want people to feel the way we feel.

We all learned about this in our Covid-19 experiences, when the world tore apart along messy politicized lines and we tried to tell whether someone was safe or not by how anxiously they masked up and maintained social distance. Anxiety became a marker of trust; if I saw you worrying at about the same level as I did, I could trust you. Whether worrying about unmasked people, or the vaccine, or any constellation in between, the stress flowed both ways. Sometimes, even if someone's specific behavior seemed congruent with ours, if they spoke too cavalierly about the risks, they might lose our trust. Because what we really wanted was that assurance of connection: to know they *felt* the same way we did. These kinds of connections are invisible most of the time, but if they are damaged, they can blow up in the drama of betrayal.

We were in Monterey on our mission trip when I stumbled upon a blowup in the youth group. Twin teenagers, Norah and Justine, were at the center of it as they sat in the church fellowship hall, waiting for dinner to be ready.

"You should have been scared," Norah said emphatically. "It was dangerous."

"It was *not* dangerous," Justine shook her head. "She was just keeping us safe."

"She was bleeding! You saw she needed a Band-Aid!"

"That was from something on her boat. The otter didn't touch her."

I sidled over to Jim and quietly asked "Who?"

Jim was keeping a low profile next to the argument, going through photos on his camera. He shook his head. "Something that happened to the leader on the kayak trip, I think. I haven't wanted to butt in."

Jim and I had been in the last boat to push off from the dock the day before when we all went kayaking. We knew we had missed a close encounter with wildlife but did not know the incident might still be bothering anyone more than twenty-four hours later.

Well, I did not mind butting in. "What happened?"

The twins turned to me swiftly, each eager for a champion to take their side.

"An otter almost turned over the guide's kayak!" Norah said, arms tightly folded in front of her.

"It did *not*. It came close and she scared it away with her paddle," Justine said, sitting back with just a hint of scorn.

"And she got hurt!" Norah piled on.

"No. She, like, cut her hand on her gear or something," Justine gestured loosely showing what a not-big-deal it was.

"Yeah, I saw it," Melvie added, in Justine's defense. "It wasn't an otter claw." She sounded disappointed, like she wished she had come so close to an otter, danger or no.

"None of you were as close to it as I was. I was in the front of the kayak. I saw it!" Norah folded her arms and sat back.

"She really wanted us to stay away from the otters," Grace said, more neutrally, trying to restore peace between her friends, "but I think it was for the otters' sake, not ours."

"She said they weigh a hundred pounds!" Norah spluttered, aghast.

"But it didn't touch anyone at all!" Justine fired back, just as upset at her sister as Norah was with the otter.

I murmured some soothing reassurances about how we had all experienced it differently, and they looked at me like I was speaking another language. They turned back to one another, and the argument raged on. The youth slowly moved into ranks as if for battle, otter-lovers on one side with Justine, and Norah on the other side with those who had also been afraid—or who, even if they themselves had not been afraid, validated Norah's fear even as they tried to soothe it. I tried sharing otter facts I looked up online and got no traction. I retreated bitterly into the kitchen, where Jim looked at me, coffee in hand, his therapist hat on for the moment, and said, "You know it isn't about the otter, right?"

Oh. Right.

It wasn't about the otter.

I fortified myself with a cup of calming tea and went back out. The main parties to this argument had stormed out of the room with an ally each, leaving the rest of the group quietly playing cards and looking anxious. I followed the sound of drama until I found them, entangled and angry on the front steps of the church.

Jim was right. It wasn't about the otter. As it turned out, it was about the fact that the twins were about to go to college. At separate colleges. One was happy to go, while the other dreaded it. They were embarking on significantly different paths, taking on new identities, and to a certain degree they were detaching, untwining their tightly woven lives. I am not saying this was an easy conversation to get through; it took hours and tears. But they were doing deep and sacred work: confessing, mending, making amends, and sharing dreams. It wasn't about the otter. It was about listening to each other and truly hearing how the other person felt. It was about fears, hopes, college, parents, work, home, boyfriends, loyalties, and that dreaded upcoming task, saying goodbye. It was about everything, really.

The otter is a sentinel species, like the sand crab. You can assess the health of the whole ecosystem if you know the health of the otters. Like the canary in the mine or the eagles affected by DDT in their prey, they warn you visibly of what may be invisible in other species. They are deeply interconnected with the other creatures of the kelp forest. They stand for everything else.

The otter was, for Justine and Norah, a sentinel experience. It stood for everything else: "If you do not feel the way I feel about the otter, how can I trust you to feel the way I feel about life?"

In our churches, the climate crisis is a sentinel issue. Young people are panicked about it, and if they see the older generation feeling anything other than panic, they feel utterly disconnected from them. Because the climate crisis stands for so many more things. Politics. Science. Truth and beauty. Justice and compassion. It stands for everything, really.

> *I'm just fully convinced that God created Covid-19 because he's trying to kill us all off and start all over. And I accept it. He can do that. That's fair. He should just try again. It's okay, we suck.*
>
> —Melvie, nineteen

In 2020, fire season started early. We had begrudgingly gotten used to the idea that we would have an annual "smoke season" in late fall, but nobody expected it to start in August any more than we had expected to still be quarantining from Covid then.

Nobody expected thunderstorms either. The weather patterns that create thunder and lightning are quite rare in California. In fact, once when we took a mission trip to Chicago and were greeted by a large thunderstorm, our California kids responded with actual panic attacks. But early on August 16, right here in the Bay Area, we were kept awake all night with rare lightning and thunder and howling wind. Limbs fell from trees on all sides, and when we awoke we found out about wildfires sparked by the lightning. Over the next few days, the wildfires grew and grew, merging with one another until we had a million-acre fire, the "August complex," which would not be fully extinguished until November. The campus of UC Santa Cruz was threatened by fire, and students were evacuated. The forests near Santa Cruz lost trees that were centuries old.

The intersections between the overlapping crises of the year were difficult to the point of absurdity. Between Covid-19 and firestorm, every aspect of life was affected. Pacific Gas & Electric took our neighborhood's power out for several days, several times, as a preemptive safety measure to reduce fire danger when high wind was predicted. So we had no power to run our air purifiers while the smoke blew in and seeped through every crack around our windows and doors. And those of us who needed electricity to learn or work from home due to the pandemic were unable to do so. Bored? None of our usual (online) coping strategies were available. During the previous year's power outages, we had managed by traveling to friends' houses in unaffected areas or by crowding into local libraries to enjoy their Wi-Fi and air-conditioning. We could not do either this year because of Covid precautions. The extroverts went out of their minds—no video chats, phone calls limited by phone battery, and even a walk in the park was now hazardous because of the air quality, though some double masked with N95s and went walking anyway. My husband and I moved the ping-pong table from the driveway to the dining room and played against the cats for a little exercise and entertainment.

We freaked out, collapsed, complained, lamented, and coped as best as we could as the electricity went off and on again. In the border neighborhoods, where some had power and some did not, people snaked extension cords over the fences so neighbors could keep their devices charged. Others bought generators, one of which exploded and burned two homes to the ground on the same block as Melvie's house. I watched the smoke, less than a mile from church, and prayed fervently as about eight fire trucks screamed up the hill. We got used to new, unprecedented levels of stress and called our doctors for tips on managing out-of-control anxiety. We raised our fists to the sky and said prayers salted with expletives, or we shrugged and told God to go ahead, wash the earth clean and start over again. We coped this way and that; we switched methods from morning to night, whenever we were at the limits of one coping method's abilities to get us through. But the last straw (of many "last straws") for many of us came on September 9, when the sun did not rise.

The smoke blew down on a high-altitude wind from Mendocino County, and we all woke up late, still hitting the snooze button at 10 a.m., not believing it could be full daytime because the light coming in through the windows looked like predawn gloom. The smoke choked the air and turned everything a terrifying orange-gray. The streetlights never went off that day, and people drove with their headlights on at high noon.

Seven-year-old McKinley came to our Godly Play class online that evening with an art project for show-and-tell. Every hour that day, she had gone to the window, looked at the sky, and found the right combination of colored pencils to match the sky. She held it up to the web camera, an accordion fold of small shaded squares. Orange, yellow, yellow-orange, orange-gray: shades of the apocalypse.

The eeriness of the brightly wrong-colored sky made many of us finally snap. Or maybe it was just that 2020 had brought us already so close to the snapping point. Even those of us who had said comfortable platitudes about getting through "these difficult times" earlier in the year now knew without a doubt that these were truly terrible times, biblical in proportion.

Fred said, "This weather sucks, but look on the bright side! It'll probably be worse next year. Enjoy it while you can." Nobody laughed.

Sam said, "What pisses me off is that it's all part of the same problem. If people would just stay where they are and live simpler lives, we wouldn't have the climate crisis, but we also wouldn't have corona. Because whether it came from bats or pangolins or whatever, it came from people living in places they didn't evolve to live in and eating things they weren't evolved to eat. Our immune systems weren't ready for corona; we'd never encountered anything like it before. This is all our fault for stepping out of our place."

Dean said, "I'm praying for the people who are poor and who don't have what they need to stay safe from the smoke and from Covid at the same time. It just isn't fair, because the richest people did the most to cause the climate crisis, but they are also the ones who can just stay home with air purifiers on. Poorer people have to go out and work and be in danger."

Naz said, "I'm not giving up on hope. I'm hanging on and trying to be optimistic. Maybe this is the wake-up call people need."

I said over and over again, "I have no words," but people kept reminding me that it was my job, as a pastor, to have words. "Lord have mercy" filled the space where other words might have been spoken. I finally found words when I heard people crying "apocalypse." *Apocalypse* was a word I could lean into, and define, and help others understand. *Apo* + *kalypto*, from the Greek: a revealing, a revelation, an unveiling of the truth. Ancient writers wrote in apocalyptic terms to tell hard truths in terrible times. Though their apocalypses may have taken form in metaphor, with great beasts and lakes of fire, they were written to reveal the violence and injustice of their world and to affirm that God's hand would rule above it all (often with a punishing vengeance). Our orange skies were an apocalypse too—not a literary one, and not written in metaphor, but a pulling back of the veils of illusion so we could quite literally see the truth around us. Finally, for many people, climate change jumped from theory to reality.

An ecological apocalypse, pulling back the curtains of denial and showing us the depth and breadth of our societal sins. Could we see it? Could we see that this was not just the hottest year on record but likely also to be the coolest year for decades to come? Could we see the way we humans had overstepped our bounds and created our own slew of problems? Could we see how the poorest people suffered the most and deserved it the least? Unfortunately, not all of us could; many people saw the skies but missed the apocalypse.

The *New York Times* ran an article about the fires that felt to me like a kick in the head. It faithfully reported on the situation but concluded that "the American West is now living through a grim version of the future."[1] I read those words and seethed hotly: we were not living through any "version of the future"; we were living through the actual present moment. It made me realize that the crisis we were experiencing was still theoretical to the editors on the East Coast. The *Times*, my old friend and mostly trusted news source, had insulted my reality, and I would not let it go.

What do you do when an apocalypse comes to you but the revelation fails to reach the people around you—whether your peers, your pastors, or your newspaper? What do you do when the devastation in your world is interpreted as "disaster is coming" rather than "disaster is already here"? When the other people just do not feel the way you feel? This mismatch of emotions feels like gaslighting, like betrayal, like being cut off in traffic (or in the lap lanes) by someone who

---

1 *New York Times* Morning Briefing, September 10, 2020.

saw you and decided to plow ahead deliberately anyway, like your kayaking partner pushing you far too close to an otter. It feels like Noah must have felt in the time before the flood, as every children's book writer has imagined it: your neighbors making fun of you for being so serious about your ark project when things really are not that bad. And suddenly you have empathy for the monstrous God of the Old Testament who is so fed up with humanity that he could just wipe them all out and start over again.

We really want people to feel the way we feel, and when they do not, the waters of our emotions roil even more. When people sit calmly by, thousands of miles away, and pontificate about the grim "future" that is our present reality without showing any trace of the panic and desperation coursing through our veins, we snap and rage. We tweet and post and find all the flaws we can to complain about. We storm out; we tell them to go to hell if they cannot listen.

Maybe I had been expecting the impossible. Maybe those who lived far away could not truly wake up to the California apocalypse unless they themselves had woken up in hell that morning, gaping at the wrong-colored sky over their own homes. Maybe the wake-up call lay deep in our animal brains, somewhere that could not be reached by a photo or even a well-researched news report, untouched by reasoning or logic. Maybe you had to be there. Still, even if our angry tweets did not reach anyone, it was important to send them; we were standing up for ourselves by saying something even if nobody listened.

Young people face this every day. The East-West betrayal I felt when the sky turned dark is just one example of the drama that swirls between the generations when those who are older look at the climate crisis with anything other than full-fledged panic. Even if the grown-ups are doing "the right thing," reducing their carbon footprint and voting for climate solutions, if they do not show that the climate crisis affects them emotionally, young people may still feel alienated.

To get through these interpersonal, interstate, intergenerational snarls of not feeling the same way others feel, we need to communicate and confront. Not as priests anymore; now we must stand up and prophesy, speaking loudly to those who are usually not listening. This may involve sending lots of never-published letters to the editor or by tweeting into the void: the joys of prophecy.

Prophets need a lot of support. When they speak to a crowd of people who do not feel the way they do, they can really use a person behind the scenes who affirms their feelings, saying, "I can only imagine that if I were in your shoes, I would feel the same way too." Even better is someone who repeats what they have said, amplifying their message, saying, "This person's experience is important information we all need to hear."

We care for people in this spiritual need by listening, empathizing, and telling them that their experience matters. We thank our ecological prophets for speaking their truth and encourage them when it seems like nobody is listening; we tell them that it was still important to express themselves clearly. We show them how speaking up can relieve the pressure that would otherwise build to a bursting point. We can also provide spiritual care by standing between parties, like

Jim helped me to do—by recognizing it was not about the otter and pointing out the deeper issues that threaten to divide us. Clear communication is the key to getting us off the rocks of resentment and releasing us from the swirls of interpersonal drama.

Chapter 17

Releasing Defensiveness

Who can detect their errors? Clear me from hidden faults.

—PSALM 19:12

The Christian religion has plenty of resources for dealing with human error. Our sacred texts provide us with dramatic stories of repentance. The stories of Jesus's life sound a radical rhythm as Zacchaeus gives reparations to the poor, as people are told to "go and sin no more," as the sons of Zebedee leave their fishing nets behind to become disciples. Saul goes from breathing threats and murder against Christians to becoming Paul, an outspoken leader in the newborn church. "You must change your life," the prophets cry from the temple courts to the city squares, calling for an end to oppression and injustice. And over the centuries the church has polished and refined our methods to help people change their lives, from formal liturgies and dramatic altar calls to intimate spiritual counseling sessions. We believe in change. But even with all these inspirations and resources, we have not discovered a cure for defensiveness.

Lashing back with defensiveness when we are challenged is a thoroughly human, natural response. When we are established in a rhythm of life, we hate to have it called into question on moral grounds. But many of us are living out of alignment with our values, ecologically speaking—particularly those of us in America, where we use an outsize proportion of the earth's resources. How can we call others to reduce their ecological impact when our own carbon footprint is so out of proportion with our ideals? Our ecological hypocrisy is like swimming across the lap lanes, cutting others off with no regard for their efforts, and making up justifications for our behavior.

We cannot move through the third spiritual need gracefully unless we can deal with our own defensiveness. If we have ideals worth striving for, we are bound to fail, but we hope someone will call us to account. If they do, though, how will we respond?

Our church challenged its members to look at our ecological impact from forty thousand feet, taking a wide-angle view, auditing our own lives, and finding ways to reduce our carbon footprints. Inspired for the journey and equipped with carbon calculators, we took off. As we ascended, many good things were revealed beneath us. Many of the church members and friends already had solar panels installed on our homes. Many of us were bikers and electric car drivers, vegetarians and actual vegans, passionate wearers of sweaters and turners-down of thermostats. The church has solar panels and uses organic local flowers in our sanctuary decor; we carpool and recycle. These things were all clear below us. But as we rose, looking at our personal carbon consumption as well as the congregation's, the larger shape of the landscape came into view. The carbon audit showed one thing that consistently doubled or even tripled a person's footprint on the earth: jet fuel.

Now, of course, pointing out our travel habits gave rise to great defensiveness. Nobody likes to get singled out. And our flying is meaningful to us, after all; our trips inform our passion for earth care. We are a relatively wealthy congregation, well educated, widely connected, with friends and family all over the globe. As a church, we host international scholars who study at the Graduate Theological Union. Later, we schedule study tours to visit these students' home countries and mission trips for the youth to connect with our partners. Thus our connections help us care about the climate crisis in far-off places. We know someone in Thailand, and that acquaintance brings the story home, emotionally speaking, when the country is hit by flooding. We are scientists who make pilgrimages to the Galápagos Islands, wildlife enthusiasts who go on safari, and humanitarians who volunteer wherever our skills are needed. We want to see the big picture, globally speaking, and it is all very noble and good. But that time spent in the air, gaining a forty-thousand-foot view of the world and its people, has been sabotaging our own best efforts to care for that same earth. When we step back and look at our carbon usage from forty thousand feet, we can watch the whole metaphor self-destruct.

I am caught in this contradiction too. In fact, I wrote much of this book on a plane. I had the first idea for this book while flying home to California from my parents' place in New York. And I pounded out many more chapters while flying to attend church conferences. What lovely irony. I wrote about the climate crisis, looking down from forty thousand feet, looking at the shining ribbons of river—delicately stretched stitches, like lace, across fields, farms, and forests—and wondering if these carefully managed ecosystems would survive four more degrees Celsius. The hypocrisy is a thrilling, urgent motivator, but still I feel defensive.

I can assuage the defensiveness with a list of my good ecological deeds: the new kinds of lightbulbs I installed, my efforts in lobbying our denomination to divest from fossil fuels, and my amateur fabric composting efforts. You can count on me to fish the recyclables out of the church's garbage bins, so help me God. But these are all small potatoes in the bigger scheme of things. And as I try to find ways to feel okay about my personal carbon footprint, I keep bumping up against those flights. I can fiddle away pounds of carbon here and there, but each flight adds upward of a ton of carbon to my footprint.

Our church published a "climate call to action" in 2021 after years of work. It asked church members and friends of goodwill in our predominantly wealthy neighborhood to (1) advocate for better climate policy, (2) reduce their food-related carbon footprint with more plant-based diets and less food waste, (3) go solar or enroll in carbon-neutral electricity programs, (4) reduce consumer consumption, especially around plastics, and (5) reduce their travel and transportation footprint. Of all these issues, traveling was the hot button. It was 2021, after all, and many of our members—particularly those who were retired—were looking forward to making up for a year of canceled travel plans as soon as their Covid-19 vaccinations kicked in. Others were concerned that such a strong stance on people's personal behavior would alienate those who felt singled out for their travel-intensive lifestyles. As a church, we had a bad history with singling people out, notably in the 1980s when a group of older church members (past childbearing age) ran a campaign against overpopulation that shamed anyone who chose to have more than two children. Young families left the church because of that campaign, and as a congregation, we vowed never to repeat that mistake. We tried to communicate encouragingly, positively, and without shame, but we found that many people still reacted with defensiveness.

Some church members professed not to have an issue with the call to reduce flying themselves but worried that other people might feel offended. Here's a secret spiritual care provider tip: when someone starts talking about what "other people" feel, they are usually having trouble with the third spiritual need. Trust has broken down, and they are stuck on the rocks. They may not have the courage to start an argument now and go through deep issues, so they warn that we will have that argument when someone else enters the conversation. Sometimes the "other people" may be entirely theoretical inhabitants of one's imagination, created just to keep things polite, but still, the underlying spiritual need is to have interpersonal accountability. We can help one another out by communicating clearly, steering toward the depths, and resisting the urge to triangulate with "other people."

Some adults particularly raised the question of how the church's challenge to reduce flying would affect the youth. "I've been all over the world," one adult member said, "and I've seen what I need to see. I can stay home now or only fly for family. But I can't bring myself to ask a young person to miss out on seeing the world."

The youth, however, took no such offense at being asked to reduce their travel. They accepted the challenge and rolled with it. They knew they could not eliminate their carbon footprint, but that it was still worth trying.

"It doesn't need to be so extreme," Justine said. "You can still go places, just try to reduce. Like maybe take one trip instead of two or three. Stay longer. Combine trips. Or find a new place you want to go that is closer. There are so many great places right here in California."

The attitude I got from the youth was that they would rather risk offending by asking for too much of an ecological commitment than deceive themselves by politely asking too little. Ask for what we need: a radical change. But change is not easy. How can we cope with feeling defensive when we are asked to change?

It was 2014 and I was only a few months into my ministry at Montclair Presbyterian Church when Suzanne showed up unannounced at the church office. She was in gardening clothes, as she had been running errands all day. She had a bag in her hand from the nursery down the block where she had gotten us some garden supplies for the little church garden. She got right down to business.

"Talitha, I'm wondering why the youth group mission trip is going to Memphis this year," she said.

"Oh! We have such great connections there," I enthused. "Two churches doing good work, and there's a wonderful organization doing such great mission in food justice and community garden access there. Did you know that Memphis is one of the hungriest cities in our nation? Plus, there's the National Civil Rights Museum, and really important history, and many of these youth haven't been to the South at all." I was excited. I had never been to Memphis myself, but one of our elders had been there for law school not too long ago, and she was giving us connections right and left. It was going to be the first mission trip I led, but I felt confident that her connections were setting me up to hit a home run.

Suzanne was smiling politely, but as I rambled on, I could tell I was not addressing whatever the issue was.

"I think it's going to be great," I finished, a little querulous. Possible complaints of all sorts rushed through my head. Too expensive? Not adventurous enough? Not religious enough? Too religious? A new pastor never likes to disappoint a parent.

Suzanne went on. "Well, those things sound wonderful. I love community gardens. And I'm sure you're going to do great work there. I'm just wondering if there wasn't a place that's closer."

"Ah, yes. We've got a new policy. Instead of going far away for the mission trip every year, we're alternating. One year close, one year far. We'll do the next trip in California; we won't fly."

"Okay. I didn't know that was a policy. Last year when they went to minister to the Hmong refugee community in Fresno, I thought that was really good, and I was hoping that was the kind of work you'd do this year too."

"Yeah, kind of a sweet spot, right? They got to meet people from far away without having to go far." I had not been on the Fresno mission trip, as it had happened right before I was hired. "But we decided to alternate between close and far so that we can also do cross-cultural trips and immerse them in another place too."

"That's fair." She looked at me apologetically. "I just wanted to let you know that I'm concerned about the carbon footprint. Dean is not old enough to go on the trip yet, but if he were, we would not be sending him."

I tried to make my face sympathetic and concerned, keeping my disappointment battened down deep inside.

"It's just not in line with what our family prioritizes," she explained.

"Oh." This objection hadn't even featured in my clamor of fears. It was 2014, and I was just barely becoming conscious of carbon counting.

"I don't know how many of the youth will end up going on the trip, but a flight to Memphis is two tons of carbon per person. That's a lot when all of you add it up."

Wow. She had done some homework. I had not. But she was gentle.

"I don't think it's wrong that you go, but wanted to raise the point. I could help research places that are closer if you'd like, for future trips. We could imagine sending him on a bigger trip someday if it's somewhere we really feel is worth the carbon it takes, but we wouldn't do it on a regular basis."

"Ok. That makes sense." Her gracious words were calming me down.

"Thanks for understanding."

"Of course. I think it's going to be a good trip. And we'll think more in the future about choosing an option closer."

We went to Memphis. We saw the food deserts. We loved helping in the community gardens. We wept at the Civil Rights Museum. We ate peanut-butter-and-banana sandwiches and really good barbecue. We met great people, admired the Mississippi River, and were inspired by the church programs we attended. We even stopped by Saint Jude's Children's Hospital, delivering fresh chard and tomatoes to their kitchen from the garden we had been weeding that morning. And then we flew home, and I kept Suzanne's feedback to myself. But it had put roots down in my brain.

The next year, our church installed solar panels. Suzanne discreetly told me that their annual carbon savings would not even make up for half of the Memphis flights. I thanked her for this reality check and kept it in mind as we all patted ourselves on the back for our good deed.

Suzanne was my priest and prophet for this work. She was clear and well boundaried in her critique, keeping the focus on what she could control, which was her family's participation. She never once mentioned "other people." But she did not stuff her critique down inside and let it become a resentment. She pointed it out in a straightforward manner and let me integrate the learning until I could see that our actions were out of line with our principles. She offered me a chance to stop and reevaluate, from the ground and not from the air.

One church's flight habits will not make or break the climate crisis. A flight's carbon contribution is huge on an individual scale but tiny on the global scale. The airline industry, the fossil fuel industry, and coal mining and fracking and refrigerants are far bigger fish to fry. Activists are leading us to make big-scale policy changes. But at the same time, we need to learn to make changes in our own lives, not just for the effect they have on the climate, but also for the effect these changes can have on us as people and on others influenced by our example. In the chaos that is not just coming but already here—from storms and fires to the reorganization of systems and industries—we need to learn how to take correction and change course. By practicing these sacred rhythms of confrontation and repentance, we can grow to become the kind of flexible, gracious people we will need to be to cope with all the changes that come.

Chapter 18
Flowing through Intersections

Once you see the forest fires that are getting worse and worse and worse, you can't close your eyes and pretend it's not happening.

—LUCIE, twenty-one

The train platform swarmed with children, teenagers, chaperones, and supportive grandmothers. Backpacks were left at home today, and the crowd was thick with signage, from rolled-up posterboards to silk-screened fabrics fluttering from poles or pinned on T-shirts. We were all on our way to the climate strike in San Francisco.

Olivia held her phone like a microphone as we got off the train. Her ambition was to interview fellow school strikers for a student podcast. As we tried to organize our small group, she went around asking people why they were here and recording what they had sacrificed or missed to get here: a test, a prep session, just a regular day of classes. Some teachers had found out how many of their students would be striking and decided to cut their losses and cancel plans, or even give the striking students a chance to earn extra credit by writing about the experience, but others stuck to plans as usual, giving their students a hard choice. We saw a teenager standing on a corner holding high a sign that said, "I'm missing a midterm but this is more important," and Olivia scurried over to get a few choice words from her about how effed up all this shit was. Carlee had brought extra cardboard and markers to share, which made our group popular. Elvin held a sign in his native Swedish, the same motto Greta Thunberg had used (*Skolstrejk för klimatet*). We were not quite done decorating the signs and so, still wielding markers and leaning on one another's backs to write, we muddled our way to the middle of Market Street, where the march began.

Organizers had planned the route around a few key locations where the climate crisis intersected with "business as usual." In front of our senator's office, an Amazon Go shop, and our local Immigration and Customs Enforcement (ICE) headquarters, tens of thousands of young people chanted and made speeches. Someone in an organizer's vest handed us small pieces of paper that mapped out the march route and gave us bullet-point explanations of each destination. We are stopping at Amazon to demand it make a more aggressive commitment to zero-emission goals. We are stopping at ICE because climate justice is migrant justice, and refugees are the most vulnerable. These pieces of paper guided and educated us. Olivia kept checking hers, grateful for the chants it suggested. "It's so good to have a specific target," she said, "not just general anger but actual doable demands." An enormous puppet show at PG&E headquarters drove home the demand for publicly owned clean energy. At BlackRock, an investment company that is the largest financial backer of fossil fuel companies, we saw employees standing in windows and on balconies idly chatting and taking pictures of the march, and the crowd surged into a new chant: "Out of the office and into the street!"

The organizers had done a great job, I thought, in directing our communication productively. We were asking for specific legislation, clean energy, divestment from fossil fuels, corporate accountability, and protections for the most vulnerable. We were being channeled in our communication as effectively as the masses of young people were being channeled from one street to another. How good it felt to know where to go and what to say, to be more or less organized as we surged down Market Street. We were learning as we went, getting into the specifics of how each corporation or public entity could stop contributing to the problems and start contributing to the solutions.

Melyssa looked at me toward the end of the march, eyes glowing, and said, "This is just so great." Thousands of people were with us. We felt like all our eco-angsty energy had been stopped up and stuck on the rocks, but when the organizers blocked off half of Market Street and sent us surging down, the vibe of the crowd was as if we had finally gotten past the rocky narrows to where the river rushed through freely. The march was a release, channeling our energy to flow for a collective purpose. We felt the joy of momentum.

We had felt a similar thrill on a smaller scale at the Monterey Bay Aquarium on our mission trip earlier that year. Not because of the joyful crowds, excited to flow through the exhibits seeing everything from otters to cuttlefish, but because of the way the aquarium and its designers educated and channeled us as we went. Huge art pieces made from salvaged plastic trash made the message as clear as any puppet show: plastic in the oceans is killing animals. The darkened rooms of the otherworldly jellyfish exhibit transported us, reminding us that the depths of the sea are as foreign and wonderful a treasure as any other planet could be. And all across the main hall of the aquarium, the planners channeled us past the lessons of history.

Many people have heard of the disastrous crash of the sardine industry in Monterey Bay. A vast amount of the United States' seafood supply was caught and processed right there on cannery row until shortly after World War II, when the sardine population disappeared. I had heard the story told as if the loss were an innocent mistake, as if the industry were just unaware that the sardine supply was exhaustible. But when I went to the aquarium, I heard the reason for this crash communicated in far starker terms. Monterey Bay had been fished sustainably for centuries beforehand, first by the Indigenous Ohlone, then by squid fishermen from China, abalone divers from Japan, and sardine fishermen from Italy. These groups had all stayed within the bay's natural limits until industry demanded more. When the military demanded canned fish to feed the troops in World War I, sustainability was no longer an important goal; the engines of war could not be denied. Between the world wars, the fish were still caught at unsustainably fast rates, now to be used as fertilizer, until the military demanded them again, at which point the bay's exploited ecosystem reached the crashing point.

The aquarium exhibit walked us through this history lesson as gracefully as the climate strike organizers walked us through the streets of San Francisco. By the end of our tour, we could see the picture clearly: you cannot oppose ecological destruction without standing against militarism too. On the other hand, the story also showed us that sustainable management of the earth's resources is not a pipe dream. It has already been practiced by many people of the global majority who preserved their Indigenous wisdom instead of leaping at the "opportunity" of industrial overextraction practices. It all connects. Our minds were suitably blown.

When our spiritual need for interpersonal accountability is unmet, we find ourselves angry without knowing who to be angry at or why. Many of us feel this way about the climate crisis: we are furious, but the fury swirls around without a target or a goal. We can help one another here by communicating as clearly as possible. It was not just anybody who overfished Monterey Bay to destruction; the race to the bottom was led by white capitalist industry, hand-in-hand with the American military. It is not just carelessness that leads us all to purchase cheap consumer goods shipped from all over the world; Amazon created this system, depending on underpaid and exploited workers, diesel-guzzling trucks, and ferociously competitive pricing. The companies most egregiously wrecking the climate are not just "the corporations." They have names, addresses, marketing departments, and strategic plans. And we are their customers. They may not listen to our complaints, but we can and should get out there in the streets, prophet style, and critique the hell out of them. By naming the societal sins that are ruining our world, we get our anger off the rocks and into the channels where we can move with momentum and freedom. The help we can offer one another here, toward the goal of interpersonal accountability, is to make our communications clearer. The more specific and accurate we can be, the better chance we have of fruitfully directing other people.

I described the feeling we had at the strike and at the aquarium to my sociologist friend, and she gave me a phrase for it. "Collective effervescence" is the feeling of doing something together. It is the graceful, easy, comfortable feeling of being attuned to others, moving together, as if we are dancing. The lightness we felt in our shoulders and our souls at the climate strike was a sign of collective effervescence at work, helping us feel that we were part of meaningful work. The weight of wisdom we began to carry as we walked through the aquarium was a more somber kind of collective effervescence, as we realized that we had been looking at just a small piece of the picture, but there was so much more to it. Whether joyful or somber, this feeling is powerful and empowering. No longer limited to our own motion, we find ourselves swept up in something bigger, riding the swells, our energy released to flow much more freely toward our goals. We benefit from the motion of the others around us, and together we find the best channels to move forward.

Postlude at Low Tide

The waves come and they crash on the beach, but then they are gone. But that water and that energy are still being held in the ocean, informing the next wave and the one after that.

—ZOE, twenty-three

I am sitting on a rock by the Monterey shore, listening to surf and splash, the soft symphony that silences the talking tourists farther back on the land. It is the last day of our mission trip, and Pastor Dan has sent us out to sit by the sea. Our job is to have some deep thoughts. "Ocean is a call to worship," we sang earlier, and ocean calls me now, not with neatly timed guitar chords but with swooshy sucking sounds, with rocks clicking together irregularly, with bubbles popping up from the sand crabs below. The sound of the ocean is as otherworldly as any heavenly angel choir. We have learned this week to look down rather than up and to imagine the divine glory revealed in the depths rather than the heights.

Dan gathered our group up and asked us twice and slowly, "How is the ocean like God?" We used tiny notebooks and pens made from recycled paper to write down our thoughts. "Go," Dan said, "and sit somewhere where what you see is not made by human hands. Think or pray or just listen for a while."

The answer comes to me right away. How is the ocean like God? It is always close at hand, yet I do not go to it often enough. Living here in the Bay Area, I am never more than an hour from the ocean (and I am much closer if you include the bay-side beaches too), yet I spend so much of my time in rooms looking at screens. I vow to change this: to go to the beach more often, to turn to God in prayer. I do not need to go far to be nurtured by an enormous, fertile, and gentle power. I just need to show up.

My focus wanders, and I survey the shore around me, making sure the group is here. Behind me I notice that Debbie has arrived; she was the last one out, having packed up her things from the kitchen. She is standing near Dan, smiling and looking satisfied at a week's work well done. I can't help thinking that the ocean and God are both like Debbie, who feeds us so abundantly.

To my right, I see that Sam has made her way to the sandy part of the beach, where she is picking up little bits of inspiration around her—the jetsam and the shells. When we gather back at the church, she will show us a handful of cigarette butts she turned up in her search and vent her righteous anger at the pollution of the ocean. Like the ocean, God calls us to help.

Nellie and Melvie have each tucked themselves between rocky extrusions to examine tide pools and fellowship with the creatures they love so much: urchins, barnacles, a single sea star. God is a home, a place of welcome for the wonderful and the strange.

Mimi has clambered surefooted over the rocks to her place of contemplation. She must be more recovered than I am from yesterday's whale watching trip. She and I had spent the whole time sick and miserable at the rail, and I am still feeling a bit shaky on my feet. Like God, the ocean is a force to be reckoned with.

Fred does not sit still for exercises like this; he is standing, braced against the changing breeze, on top of the largest rock looking out on the vastness of it all. God is far, far beyond all our knowing.

I cannot see the rest of the group, but I trust they are where they need to be, each finding the place that works for them. The ocean is ever-changing, and each of us can see only a part of it.

Something in the water catches my eye. It is an otter, here to remind me of the lessons I have learned. As Anne Lamott says, God is such a show-off. I was hard-hearted when I arrived here a week ago, but yes, of course I fell in love with the otters. They made their way into my heart as expertly as they pry open the shellfish they eat. The baby otters at the aquarium were irresistible; they reminded me of our kittens as they rolled and wrestled with their toys. The adult otters we kayaked past in the wild were no less adorable for all their hundred-pound ferocity. But most of all, it was the story of the otters that got me. Everyone in Monterey wanted to tell this story: the church members, the aquarium guide, the kayak instructor. They told of how the otters had been hunted for their fur and were thought to be extinct. But in 1938, not too far from Monterey, a population of fifty otters was discovered and protected. Like Noah's family coming off the ark, they eventually repopulated the whole area. Humans of all kinds helped them to this end: scientists monitored their populations, conservation activists won refuges for them in the Environmental Protection Act, neighbors shepherded orphan pups off the beaches and into a surrogacy program at the aquarium, and artists designed stuffed animals to endear the otters to future generations. With all this passionate support, they survived, and there are now about three thousand otters off the coast of California. They are not safe yet. A single oil spill could take the entire population back down to desperate levels. And their food sources are threatened as the climate crisis changes the temperature and acidity of their watery home. Their future is in peril. But spending time with the otters is like spending time with a cancer survivor, someone who has been to the end of the world and back again. It is like telling the Passover story: "Our ancestors were slaves in Egypt." When I think about ecological work, the otters' survival gives me courage to keep trying.

There is fog on the water today. You cannot see across to the cliffs of Santa Cruz, where Linnea does her fieldwork, but my mind places them, in faith, where I think they will be when the fog burns off. Even farther out to sea, in the embrace of the fog, are the humpback whales who swam around our boat yesterday, massive and mesmerizing, with the seals and birds who follow them when they feed. Out there life goes on, desperate and fragile, rich and resilient. God is magnificent.

We will go home today. Tomorrow we will each stand for a few minutes in the pulpit and tell our congregation what we learned. We will be going home with far more than our Blue Theology notebooks and our handwritten affirmation journals. We have our pocketsful of beach glass and shells, our photos of the whales and seals and otters, and some new-found spiritual strength. Yesterday's otter argument gave me, at least, an upgrade in my confidence that we as a group can work through big issues together. We have all refined our trash-removal habits and our sense that we can do important work bit by bit. And we will all take the memory of this foggy embrace with us: the goodness of the ocean, the delight of being alive, of being part of such an incredible world.

In the fall we will march in the climate strike in San Francisco, shortly before fire season arrives and outdoor activities get canceled for the sake of our lungs. Next winter the banners we made will arrive, stitched and finished by Kimberly. We will hang them in our sanctuary and remember what was most important.

Next year the ocean will be a little warmer, a little higher, and a little more acidic, and the otters will have to work a little harder to find their food. Next year the fires will start earlier and burn hotter and farther. Next year our cries will become a little more desperate for climate action, and some of us will decide to go vegan, to stop flying entirely, to divest and boycott and protest.

But I vow to remember to go to the ocean. Not to spend all my time in rooms on screens fighting the good fight, but to make the short pilgrimage to these waters, to spend some time in their wild and wise presence. God is always there for us, in the mystery, in the change, in the constancy. Glory to God in the deepest.

Acknowledgments

My friend Ariel asked me one New Year's Day to list five big things I could do and made me write them down on paper and checked up on my progress until they were accomplished, including this book. Thank you, Ariel, for that interpersonal accountability.

My husband, Michael, asked, "What if we have a writing group every Friday night?" and put up with my bad attitude until I finally started enjoying myself. Brian, Ariel, and Renee joined us. The cats sat on our laps and laptops. Thank you, my dear writing group; you taught me to take delight in the process.

Michael's creativity overflows in the house we share, and from him I have learned many ways to trick myself into writing. Thank you for all the nights you challenged me to do "any nonzero amount" of writing before bed and the times you told me a shitty first draft would do. Thank you for all the abundant ideas you gave me and for your love, which changed me. You are a constant inspiration to me, and your help with this book has been invaluable.

The baby deserves thanks of a sort too. Ziggy, someday you will read this, and I will tell you again about how I finished writing the book while nursing you in various positions. Thanks for your flexibility.

Rozella Haydee White, the Love Big coach, encouraged me like a momma bird pushing the fledgling out to fly. Thank you, Rozella, for your strong faith when I did not know I was ready.

My boss and neighbor and friend Ben Daniel oriented me to the world of publishing like a traveler in a foreign land. He advocated for my work at the church by establishing that writing *is* ministry and normalizing the use of study leave funds for writing classes and mobile keyboards. Thank you, Ben, for your mentoring.

Beth Gaede was the editor of my dreams, believing in the book, coaxing it out in the tricky places, and constantly asking me to define my terms. Thank you, Beth, for all the fun we had together.

Linnea, Lucie, Zoe, and Suzanne read early drafts and guided me. Thank you for your wisdom.

When I was young, I went to "Take Your Daughter to Work Day" at CBS, where my news-writer father, Tom Phillips, gave me a thirty-three-second script and asked me if I could make it thirty seconds. The writing lessons continue to this day, and he spent weeks helping me tighten the book up before deadline. Thank you, Dad, for your talent, experience, and commitment to the craft of writing. No, you can't shorten this paragraph.

Thank you to the Christian Church (Disciples of Christ) in Pacific Grove, who offer Blue Theology to the world. You are an inspiration and a beacon of hope.

Most of all, thank you to the good people of Montclair Presbyterian Church. The climate action committee, the activists, the poets, the children, the parents, especially the youth: you who mourn and lament, measure and calculate, install solar panels and cook vegan meals. Thank you for your passion, for "holding on to what is good," for correcting me, for leading us. Thank you for sharing your raw feelings and allowing me to publish them. May our work be a blessing to the world.